HEALING THE WOUNDS of the DISPLACED

HEALING THE WOUNDS of the DISPLACED

Pastoral Ministry in Immigrant Churches

FRANCISCO ZAMORA AVILA

FORTRESS PRESS
MINNEAPOLIS

HEALING THE WOUNDS OF THE DISPLACED
Pastoral Ministry in Immigrant Churches

Copyright © 2025 Fortress Press. All rights reserved. Except for brief quotations in critical articles or reviews, no part of this book may be reproduced in any manner without prior written permission from the publisher. Email copyright@fortresspress.com or write to Permissions, Fortress Press, PO Box 1209, Minneapolis, MN 55440-1209.

Library of Congress Control Number: 2025009652 (print)

Cover design: Brice Hemmer
Cover image: Church in Choucha refugee camp—stock photo from Philippe Lissac/Getty Images

Print ISBN: 979-8-8898-3281-2
eBook ISBN: 979-8-8898-3282-9

This book is dedicated to all those pilgrims who, due to life circumstances, leave everything behind in their lands in search of a better life; resilient people who face any challenge in search of new horizons. May God continue to use you to create, make, and build wonderful works.

Praise for *Healing the Wounds of the Displaced*

Framed within Francisco Zamora Avila's own experience as an undocumented immigrant during most of his life, and based on his journey as an undocumented theological student and pastor for immigrant communities, *Healing the Wounds of the Displaced* offers us first a fresh account of the historical background and present-day realities of Hispanic/Latino undocumented populations. After summarizing the contributions of key Hispanic theologians to a "biblical theology of migration" and describing the psychological needs of the immigrant community, he invites us to consider what he sees as the new dimensions for doing pastoral ministry with those "in the margins." This invitation cannot be more pertinent for Christian leaders in this country who, independent of their political and theological positions, strongly believe in a God who "protects the strangers who live in our land."

—**Fernando Cascante**, senior consultant with the Calvin Institute of Christian Worship

Amid the multiple controversies surrounding immigration, the voice of an undocumented pastor calling for the church to minister effectively and faithfully to his community is a unique and essential contribution to the conversation. Pastor Zamora Avila's reflections are raw and real. Whether we agree or not, we need to listen.

—**Alexia Salvatierra**, academic dean, Centro Latino, Fuller Theological Seminary

What would a pastoral approach to immigration, written by an immigrant working among immigrants on the front lines of ministry, look like? Zamora Avila gives us not only a realistic picture of such ministry and its challenges, but a hopeful way to embody an ecclesiology of accompaniment and solidarity with immigrant neighbors today. Weaving together relevant demographics, storytelling, theological reflections, and pastoral experience, Zamora Avila puts a human face on the traumas experienced by immigrant neighbors, their hunger for belonging, and the church's call to attend to their holistic needs and rejoice in their gifts.

—**Leopoldo A. Sánchez M.**, professor of systematic theology, Concordia Seminary, and author of *Sculptor Spirit* (IVP Academic, 2019) and *Immigrant Neighbors among Us*, coedited with M. Daniel Carroll R. (Pickwick, 2015)

Francisco brings to light the plight of the immigrant through his incredible personal journey and vulnerability. This material is a must-read for those in church leadership who desire a compassionate, Christ-honoring way to embrace the immigrant. It's also a must-read for those church leaders who aren't so sure how to respond to the immigrant in Christ. It is both compelling and practical!

—**James Gann**, founder and director of Manna

Contents

	Preface	ix
	Introduction: New Ecclesial Models for an Immigrant Church	1
1.	Defining the Immigrant Community	23
2.	A Theology That Invites Immigrants into Belonging	45
3.	Psychological Needs in the Immigrant Community	73
4.	Pastoral Care in the Margins	95
	Conclusion	115
	Epilogue	119
	Notes	123
	Bibliography	135

Preface

My experience as an undocumented student often made me wonder whether it was worth continuing pursuing a master's degree or if I should quit the seminary. This questioning was never because I did not love the seminary, but because there were times when I did not have the financial resources to continue. In my case, because of my status, receiving a student loan was not an option; therefore, the struggle to be able to pay for each class was even harder. My status deprived me of thinking that I could achieve a degree, and, at that time, I couldn't see the point in continuing to invest in my education.

My undocumented status also affected the way I projected myself as a minister. I did not see any splendid future for me and my ministry, because the reality was that I was an undocumented pastor who a couple of years earlier had planted a church, without any denominational support. After a couple of years of launching the ministry, I was still waiting for my small ministry to consolidate and flourish. In addition to that, Covid-19 pandemic hit, and it came to change the way we traditionally practiced our faith.

During the pandemic, 90 percent of the employees where I worked were laid off. I remember very long days at work during that time, with a lot of fear and distress, because as an undocumented worker, the last thing I wanted was to lose my job. Especially, as the main breadwinner, I wanted to make sure my family was financially well. There are many memories of me rushing to get off work, because I had to broadcast our virtual service, and then continue with my assignments for the seminary and be able to graduate.

PREFACE

It was a complicated stage, being an undocumented student, undocumented pastor, and undocumented worker all at once. However, God amazed me, and what seemed lifeless, today feels like an invigorating adventure. Currently, I have finished my master's degree, the ministry survived after Covid-19, and God has sent amazing people my way to reach this moment where I'm here trying my best to write a book in a foreign language.

The dream of writing a book was born at the seminary. At first, I did not take it seriously because I thought it was the excitement of having such excellent professors and because I was experiencing everything that the academic world entails. Little by little the ideas in my mind were refined, and I really wanted to carry out that desire. After I finished my master's degree, I thought that my dream would take much longer to fulfill. Melancholy took hold of me, because I thought that moving away from academia would take me even further away from being able to write a book. It was not until 2022, when, at a pastor's retreat with Manna SoCal where I met Dr. Chris Adams that I felt hope. In one of our group sessions, he listened to my story and advised me not to let my dream die. His words encouraged me, and with his experience, he provided me with the information and necessary tools to work on what became the beginning of the dream.

God has used many people who have blessed me in different stages of my life. Dr. Adams is just one of the wonderful people I have met. It is impossible for me to name everyone; however, I want to thank all those who know me; thank you for being part of my life. I thank Natalie, my beloved wife, the woman who dared to take the risk of marrying an undocumented immigrant like me. Marrying an undocumented immigrant has its implications and limitations in many aspects. Thank you for believing in me, for your support and love, and your patience.

Esteban and Glenda, thank you very much for always being there and accompanying me since the beginning of the ministry. You have always given Natalie and me your unconditional support and you are always patient to listen and advise us. James and Charlie, we love you guys. Only you know how crucial it has been for us and the ministry to have met you. You are the ones who helped us shape what is the focus of our ministry today, and the ones who have taught us another way of doing church.

Finally, I would like to thank Laura Gifford and Fortress Press. Laura, you have helped me edit this work. You have literally given me a voice. I know that due to my language limitations you have worked harder than usual. Additionally, you have had the patience to help me communicate what I wanted to say. Thank you very much for believing in me, in my story, and for guiding me from the beginning in this project. All of this has been new, but your cordiality, professionalism, and patience has made my dream come true. Fortress Press, thank you for being a platform that gives scope to our voices.

Introduction
New Ecclesial Models for an Immigrant Church

The issue of immigration has become one of the most controversial issues in recent presidential elections. Unfortunately, partisan political enthusiasm has sometimes triumphed over attention to where God is calling us and caused conflicting opinions in some sectors of the American church. However, there are many scholars crafting serious reflections on the subject and its implications for Christianity in the United States. It would be a mistake for the American church to ignore the changes that immigration is generating in this era, in a nation that has historically been considered a nation of immigrants.

The current crisis happening at the border between Mexico and the United States should lead us to deeply consider the role we have to play as a hosting church witnessing this phenomenon. Immigration, as complex and as polarizing as it can be, is a phenomenon calling for us as a church to pause and intentionally reflect on what immigration's role is in God's story and its purpose for the churches in this nation.

Unfortunately, this is not an easy topic to address because of all the elements involved in the migration spectrum and US policy. This topic gives rise to many emotions and feelings in most of us. It raises tensions, and unfortunately, when politicized, it creates divisions. Therefore, I humbly propose to address this issue from a pastoral perspective. I ask you to please set aside any position or ideal that stops you from reflecting on immigration as an opportunity for pastoral work. After all, and at the end of any debate or discussion on this topic, our purpose as a church does not change; in one way or another we must announce God's love to all humanity. I hope that through this lens we can discover the heart of the immigrant community: a community often ignored, and therefore very misunderstood. Being an immigrant, whether by choice or any other reason, is not something easy to assimilate. The heart of the immigrant experiences many needs in each stage of this journey. In addition, my desire is also to honor the love and passion of those who accept, care for, and help this community in the different emerging ministries of the United States.

When you start looking deeply into the heart of the people that have been displaced, you will find a soul plundered by suffering and uncertainty. It is a wounded heart that has been exposed to horrible things in the search for a better life. In many cases, the suffering is so tremendously distressing that it can lead to changes in one's behavior or affect one's personality and alter one's perception of self. For the displaced, it is an inner wound that hurts or even kills, destroying them from the inside.

When immigrants begin their journey to the United States, many of them leave not only family behind, but also part of themselves behind. They need to come to terms with the idea that they will no longer be able to communicate in their mother tongue, or celebrate their culture, nor find refuge in their motherland. They will need to leave life behind as they know it and begin the grueling journey to the border. If they are lucky enough to cross the border alive, many of them still walk for days in the mountains or desert. If they are not able to keep up with the group's pace, they are left behind to their own devices. The Mexican side of the border is a dangerous place, and the displaced become the most vulnerable due to criminal activity like drug cartels fighting for territory. In many instances, immigrants are threatened and forced to carry drugs into the United States. The *coyotes* (smugglers) might use them as mules to transport drugs across the border. Unfortunately, human trafficking is also a reality at the border, and the outsiders, especially women, become prey to organized crime. At the border, they can easily be assaulted, kidnapped, raped, and killed. I remember when I became a victim of one of these crimes. Back in 1999, when I was planning to cross the border, the group I was with was assaulted when we arrived in Tijuana, Mexico. Someone barged into our hostel and robbed us at gunpoint. Unfortunately, these dangers are only an introduction to the many challenges of an immigrant's new life. Once an immigrant manages to overcome these dangers and makes it into the United States, they often live in low income and marginalized neighborhoods, and due to a lack of financial stability, they are forced to share dwellings with strangers.

The detachment experienced by migrants disrupts their family relationships; it affects their mental health and creates negative long-term effects and emotional distress. In addition, it negatively affects their identity, which creates self-esteem problems. Being exposed to an unwelcoming host culture may lead to psychological disorders, isolation, or other mental health issues. They lose their sense of belonging to a community and enter a path of depression and loneliness because of the *illegal* or *alien* role they are labelled with. On their journey toward the American dream, they become voiceless and invisible to the system. Therefore, fear and distrust prevent them from starting a healthy process of assimilation and acculturation.

Living in the United States as an undocumented immigrant means living a life of constant stress and anxiety. We know that there is always the possibility of being separated from our loved ones through deportation. We can be victims of racial profiling, suffer derogatory treatment due to prejudice, or experience other ills. For example, in about thirty states here in the United States, immigrants cannot obtain a driver's license.[1] Generally, we are not eligible for health care or health insurance, and if we get any coverage, it is usually minimal and at a high cost. We can have a well-paying job, or even establish a small business, yet still be in the shadows of the system and government. Deep within ourselves there is also an incessant fear that due to our immigrant status, our dreams may never be achieved. For example, due to our status and ineligibility to receive student loans, we may be unable to pursue higher education. Consequently, our dreams of owning our own home and creating a better life may never be attainable. Due to these issues, we are forced to become residents living in the margins of society. We live with a longing for freedom and acceptance, but are often left wounded, frustrated, and vulnerable to an array of grievances.

As an undocumented immigrant myself, I have experienced firsthand a lot of the grievances immigrants face on their journey to assimilation. Many of these issues revolve around seemingly simple tasks yet can be immensely stressful. One of those issues is the language barrier. It is frustrating to want to express ideas or emotions and not be able to articulate and express them properly because one doesn't speak the language. Unfortunately, the language barrier is only part of the problem of being displaced.

This book is centered on those who are displaced because of the migration phenomenon. The term *displaced* refers to immigrants both documented and undocumented, and refugees. In this book, however, I will be referring specifically to the undocumented immigrant when using the term *displaced*. This book focuses on the context of the United States where I have lived for more than twenty-four years now, with twenty-three of those years as an undocumented immigrant myself. Although some other ethnic groups will be mentioned, my focus is the Hispanic[2] or Latin American people, noting that, "while Latin American migrants come from many countries, you become a Hispanic in the United States."[3]

MY IMMIGRATION JOURNEY

I arrived in this country as a teenager. After my arrival, I started experiencing the losses and psychological effects caused by my migration journey. When leaving my homeland, my age and naivety did not allow me to understand the implications of the decision I had made and the dangers I would soon experience. I remember the excitement and enthusiasm of coming to the United States. The illusion of coming to this country did not allow me to perceive and fully understand the wounds and damage caused by my departure, especially to my mother and family who stayed behind.

As I started my journey, I soon realized that the magical idea presented to me by those who come *para el norte* was not as it seemed. It was not a fairytale or a simple task. After I crossed the border, I ended up being tremendously affected, even traumatized, as I dealt with depression and anxiety issues. Sadly, this is common to the immigrant experience.

In my case, I almost lost my life at the border. I was lost in the mountains for about three days, without food and with only one dollar in my pocket. When I was lost in the mountains, I remember that I prayed to God: "If you get me there, I promise to go to church to thank you." A day after that prayer, I found my guide, who had managed to escape from the persecution of the border patrol a couple days prior. After a few weeks, I finally arrived in Los Angeles. My cousin picked me up; my dad had already paid the *coyote*, so it was just a matter of picking me up at any gas station. A few days later, my cousin took me to church, and I went to fulfill my promise. It was Wednesday night in a small church in East Los Angeles and before ending his sermon the pastor made a call to the altar. I went to the altar to give thanks, and after that day, my spiritual life changed, not my legal status, but my heart.

I was a fifteen-year-old boy from a small town in Hidalgo, Mexico, who had no idea of the changes I would experience. I belonged to a very disadvantaged household in Mexico, but I was not used to paying rent, much less having my own relatives charging me for everything from food to gas. That was very hard to assimilate, as Hispanic families tend to support each other as an entire family, not just focusing on the central household members. *Familismo*,[4] *personalismo*,[5] and *respeto*[6] are values very common in most Hispanic family structures.

For me to fulfill those demands, I needed to find a job, but it was not an easy task. My physical appearance did not reflect adulthood, but rather I still looked like a child. It was extremely hard; I felt as if nobody supported me to study, or at the very least give me the opportunity to take classes to learn to speak English. It still hurts me to look back at that stage of my journey. I can't help but think, "if only someone had supported me, surely I would have done better."

I noticed huge changes in my personality. I became shy, quiet, and isolated myself. I cried every day. After a couple of months, I found a job, and that income helped me provide for my family in Mexico and pay my expenses here in the United States. I have always wanted to continue studying, so I decided to attend adult school to learn English. With a lot of sacrifice, I finished the ESL program. Later, I would understand exactly how complicated it was for an undocumented person to attain a higher education. When I was about to enroll in a community college, I found out that for *international* students, the cost of classes was sadly just too high; minimum wage was not enough to cover that expense.

After living for fourteen years in the United States I became an undocumented pastor. The process of discovering my calling included several years of involvement in my local church and a few years at a Bible Institute. My ingenuousness and lack of experience did not prepare me to understand the challenges that the church faced as an institution in recognizing and ordaining me as a pastor. For me, the church had become a refuge that transcended status and anything against the dignity of any human being. At that time, it was complicated for the different denominations to ordain undocumented immigrants. After finishing my bachelor's degree in Christian ministry, I confirmed my call to the ministry.

I never imagined answering the call would be such a lonely process. At that time, the community life of the church had helped me fill any family emptiness I felt, and being actively involved in church had helped me develop and recover my personality, which was affected by my migration journey. The church was home, family, and citizenship. This was a period when the only safe space I had as an undocumented immigrant was invaded by doubt and suspicion. A stage full of questions regarding the church, this was a tough process, very difficult to assimilate. It was a mixture of ecclesiastical distrust and denominational disillusionment. It was difficult for me to articulate the idea of the church being unable or unwilling to truly reaffirm the dignity of the undocumented. Those were the events and experiences that led me to wonder if we were doing enough as a church. Because of my formation at the seminary and incorporation into ministry, I realized there was an enormous disconnect between the church and the plight of the displaced. Although the topic has gained relevance in this time, we still need new models of doing ministry that can lead us to action and pastoral work among this community.

I strongly believe that part of this disconnection has to do with an unawareness of the realities that this community lives in, such as the unfamiliarity and profound impact of migration on their wellbeing. My purpose throughout this work is to answer the following five questions: (1) Why are new ecclesial models necessary? (2) Who are we serving? (3) How might we craft a theology that is better equipped to support this community? (4) What psychological support does this community need? (5) What does pastoral ministry on the margins look like?

My hope is to create awareness within the American church so we can create new pastoral models to better serve this community. It is an invitation to reflect on how immigration is changing the way we do *Ekklesia*, and how the pastoral ministry requires new elements when accompanying this vulnerable community. I intend to spark curiosity and creativity to incorporate new elements into our ministries' consciousness toward the struggles of the displaced community.

WHY ARE NEW ECCLESIAL MODELS NECESSARY?

In order to answer this question, we must first take a look at immigration in politics and church dynamics. In 1999, when I migrated to the United States, George W. Bush was the strongest candidate for the presidency, and part of his propaganda addressed comprehensive immigration reform. He proposed to change the character of the Immigration and Naturalization Service to make America more welcoming to new immigrants.[7] At that time, I was working in the fields, where all the employees were immigrants.

Hearing Bush's proposals on immigration brought a lot of expectation and excitement to this voiceless community, especially for immigrant who arrived after 1986.[8] I can assure you that at least in the fruit-picking fields, there was hope and happiness about the possibility of finally experiencing freedom. According to the Pew Research Center, the undocumented immigrant population has grown rapidly since 1990, reaching a peak of 12.2 million in 2007.[9]

In early 2000, when President Bush came into office, he started meeting with Mexican President Vicente Fox and engaging in migration discussions.[10] Unfortunately, those glimpses of hope abruptly disappeared because of the terrorist attacks on September 11, 2001. Terrorism became the reason why the American way of thinking suddenly shifted its perspective on immigrants and security at the border became a national priority. New restrictive policies appeared, multiple security concerns were addressed, and new laws were approved that have left a great impact on immigration.

The Patriot Act (2001) broadened the scope by which the United States could deny admission to suspects. The fear of being vulnerable at certain border areas and ports of entry led United States law enforcement and national security agencies to scrutinize individuals, imposing restrictions on arriving aliens and asylum seekers. In addition, Congress enacted the Homeland Security Act (2002), which led to a significant restructuring of federal agencies. The government organized these agencies to work under the umbrella of the newly created Department of Homeland Security.[11] At this time, most of the US population was filled with fear and uncertainty, and, feeling vulnerable; they were willing to do anything to secure the borders. Not surprisingly, there was a significant uprising in church attendance after the attacks, as Americans were concerned about the future.[12]

After September 11 there were no major considerations of a comprehensive immigration reform for several years. It was not until May

2006 that the Comprehensive Immigration Reform Act was approved by the full Senate. The act included provisions to strengthen border security with fencing, vehicle barriers, surveillance technology, and more personnel; a new temporary worker visa category; and a path to legal status for immigrants in the country illegally if they met specific criteria. But the bill was never taken up by the House.[13] The Hispanic community was truly disappointed to see politicians from one party increase their anti-immigration rhetoric while the other party went out of their way to avoid the whole issue.[14] In all, the Bush era was marked by mixed messages regarding immigration.

Regarding the American church, during this era, some denominations and non-denominational churches made statements regarding immigration reform, and the American church, including many evangelicals, experienced a time of progressive action regarding immigration. Some Black Protestant organizations and leaders remained silent, while Hispanic communities started raising their voices about the issue. Rev. Romal J. Tune addressed this lack of support toward immigration from Black organizations in a post on HuffPost.[15] Among other factors, some argue that African American Churches, unlike the Catholic Church and other Protestant denominations, do not have advocacy offices in Washington, DC, and that many of their websites offer very limited public advocacy guidance in general, which reduces their visibility, especially in this type of affair.[16]

In October 2006, the National Association of Evangelicals (NAE) issued a resolution on immigration: "As a people of faith we support immigration reform that reflects human dignity, compassion, and justice integral to a nation under God." Later, in 2009, the NAE released "Immigration 2009," a call to Christians to show compassion and hospitality to migrants. The document was divided into three major sections: Biblical foundations, national realities, and a call to action. The first section acknowledges that all humans, including immigrants, are made in the image of God. The second section is a call to the nation to maintain the integrity of the national borders, address the situation of millions of undocumented immigrants, create a realistic program to respond to labor needs, and manifest the humanitarian spirit that has characterized the United States. The last section states, "We believe that national immigration policy should be considerate of immigrants who are already here." [17]

Many denominations continued to produce their own documents. In 2006, the Southern Baptist Convention (SBC) issued a resolution titled "On the Crisis of Illegal Immigration." The document calls on the federal government to address immigration because of the crisis at the border. It was also a call for Christians to follow biblical principles in caring for migrants and meeting the needs of the immigrant communities. In 2011, the SBC resolution "On Immigration and the Gospel" addressed similar themes as the 2006 one; however, it declares "this resolution is not to be construed as support for amnesty for any undocumented immigrant."[18]

The Christian Reformed Church (CRC) issued a report in 2009 titled "Committee to Study the Migration of Workers." It is a call for comprehensive immigration reform. The report also calls for increased opportunities for unauthorized aliens to legalize their status.[19] In 2012, the Evangelical Immigration Table (EIT) was created to support immigration reform based on six principles: (1) respect human dignity; (2) unity of the immediate family; (3) respect for the rule of law; (4) security of national borders; (5) fairness to taxpayers; and (6) legalization of unauthorized aliens.[20] Their position does not represent "left" or "right," but rather a mindful and prudent consideration of what their faith requires for all Christians and what serves the nation best.[21]

In 2008, Barack Obama was elected the first African American president of the United States. His main concern was health care reform; however, his charisma and good rhetoric quickly won the hearts of minorities and revived the hope for a comprehensive immigration reform. According to his administration, "The Hispanic community played an integral part of that plan to win the future."[22] Obama's rhetoric and personality caused many moderate evangelicals to vote for the Democratic Party for the first time in their lives. As an undocumented immigrant, I was very confident about the idea of comprehensive immigration reform under Obama's administration.

Nevertheless, under his administration 2.5 million undocumented immigrants were deported. To the misfortune of undocumented immigrants, instead of being their champion, he was instead labeled as the *Deporter in chief*.[23] In 2011 alone, 396,906 immigrants were deported, the highest number of deportations ever; 216,698 had been convicted of crimes, including 44,653 convicted of drug related crimes, 35,927 convicted of driving under the influence, 5,848 convicted of sexual offenses, and 1,119 convicted for homicide. The rest of the deportations were a result of routine traffic stops, immigrants using forged documents, or as part of a crackdown on employers who hired undocumented workers.[24]

Out of those 396,906 deported in 2011, 22 percent were the parents of children who were American citizens. More than five thousand of those children were placed in foster care because of the deportation of their parents. Some children were put up for adoption once the state courts ruled that they were abandoned by their parents due to deportation, even though the current guidelines call for making exceptions for children with deported parents. The lack of legal representation and the impediment of being unable to communicate effectively due to language barriers make it difficult for many to defend their case.[25]

During Obama's second term, between 2012 and 2014, he introduced the Development, Relief, and Education for Alien Minors Act, known as the DREAM Act, a proposal to offer legal status to children brought to the United States illegally as minors; however, it failed to pass Congress. Simultaneously, President Obama pushed for the Deferred Action on Childhood Arrivals (DACA) policy to protect undocumented individuals under the age of sixteen arriving in the United States and allow them to apply for temporary permits. About 900,000 young individuals became potential beneficiaries of this policy.[26] DACA is the closest thing to a legal residency for many of the DREAMERS. They are protected from deportation for two years, and some may even receive their work permit after meeting their eligibility requirements. Although the status does not grant a long-term immigration status, it does protect the beneficiaries until the immigration laws change.[27] When I applied for DACA, my application was denied because I had no way to prove that I arrived in the United States before June 1999. I was not able to adjust my status until I applied through my wife in 2014.

In 2013, the Senate passed a Comprehensive Immigration Reform bill. It was a proposal for a 13-year process to citizenship. However, for a variety of reasons, the House did not consider the Senate bill. By 2014, the rise of a new crisis at the border contributed to legislative hesitation. Thousands of Central American unaccompanied minors crossed the border.[28] Finally, in that same year, former President Obama tried to expand DACA, but his initiatives did not pass in court. During the Obama administration, a growing number of evangelical leaders and organizations started getting involved in the immigration issue, speaking out against massive deportations. A small group of those leaders finally became a bit more vocal, and they started bringing awareness to the issue. Hispanic evangelicals continued to lead at this time and Asian voices began to arise, though black evangelicals remained silent.[29] As we can see, Christians have contributed to the public policy debate on immigration by raising awareness of the system's shortcomings and promoting a comprehensive reform.

By 2015, the United States started experiencing a time of fragmentation, polarization, and controversy. Political ideologies began to fuel a growing anti-immigrant sentiment; its climax occurred when Donald Trump used immigration as a cornerstone in his presidential campaign. After Trump's election in 2016, hate crimes against Hispanics increased 176 percent compared with the previous average. Trump linked migration with terrorism and used harsh comments about Mexicans like: "They are not our friends, believe me. They're bringing drugs. They're bringing crime. They're rapists. And some, I assume, are good people."[30] Trump's campaign began with a call to build a monumental wall and deport millions of undocumented immigrants already living in the United States. The argument of his rhetoric was that undocumented immigrants were taking American jobs from people and bringing crime. At that time, the situation became more polarized than ever. However, an undocumented immigrant from Latin America is more likely to be someone who loves God than to be a murderer.[31] Since then, the term *Trump Effect* has been coined by psychologists to describe the notable increase in racialized, xenophobic, homophobic, and transphobic bullying in schools since the presidential election of Donald Trump.[32]

In addition, Trump lowered the annual number of refugees accepted from 97,000, in 2016, to approximately 50,000 in 2017. By 2018, the formal cap was 45,000. The administration tried to build a short wall in the Santa Ana reserve along the Texas-Mexico border. Trump also attempted to increase the number of agents for the US Immigration and Customs Enforcement (ICE) agency and eventually overturned Obama's executive order on DACA in September 2017, with an expiration date of March 5, 2018. The Trump administration had zero tolerance, prosecuting any adult who crossed the border illegally by labeling their actions as criminal; families were separated, and about 2,300 children were separated from their families.[33]

I still remember the 2016 presidential campaign; for an undocumented immigrant, it was a time of frustration, anxiety, and anger. The negative declarations fired up an already well-established stigma of the immigrant community. I remember a Hispanic pastor sharing how his family was verbally attacked in the parking lot of a grocery store as a Caucasian male shouted at them saying, "Go back to your country." By the time we started hearing more news about raids taking place in various workplaces, I was afraid of not returning home and was frightened with thoughts of the possibility of getting deported.

Under the Trump administration, Black Protestant leaders and denominations increasingly started raising their voices against the president's initiatives on immigration. Nevertheless, according to Christianity Today, about 80 percent of white evangelicals voted for Trump in 2016 and again in 2020. His evangelical allies, convened by friend and televangelist Paula White, included leaders such as First Baptist Dallas pastor Robert Jeffress, Gateway Church pastor Robert Morris, and Samaritan's Purse president Franklin Graham.

Some evangelical leaders who protested Trump throughout the 2016 election, such as Southern Baptist Theological Seminary president Albert Mohler, ended up backing him in 2020. Their support was based on Trump's support of religious liberty, banning of abortion, and other issues. Evangelicals who were white, over fifty-five years old, and weekly church attendees were most likely to agree with such positions, considering Trump kept his promises to support matters important to faithful Christians.[34]

That negative attitude and hostile environment toward the displaced community prompted the development of multiple faith-based organizations whose purpose was to accompany, protect, and advocate for the immigrant community. In Southern California, organizations such as Matthew 25, We Care, La Voice, United Methodist Congregation Network, Southern California Immigration Task Force of the Catholic, and Clergy and Laity United for Economic Justice (CLUE) created resistance movements to defend immigrants and promote their well-being in the face of harmful government policies.[35] These have been perhaps the most important social movements since the launch of the Sanctuary Movement in 1982. That earlier movement was launched in Los Angeles in response to reports of the deplorable conditions in immigration detention centers.

Some Protestant churches have been politically engaged regarding immigration. In 2004, for example, the Presbyterian Church (PCUSA), approved a report titled "Comprehensive Legalization Program for Immigrants Living and Working in the United States."[36] In 2012, they adopted two resolutions: the first one is a call to make the welfare of immigrants and unauthorized migrants a priority and the second offers advice "On Advocating for Comprehensive Immigration Reform."[37]

In 2006 the general convention of the Episcopal Church approved a report, "The Alien Among You,"[38] which called on Christians to welcome strangers and encouraged them to support immigration reform. Then, in 2010, they released a theological study on immigration: "The Nation and the Common Good: Reflections on Immigration Reform."[39] This study explores the relationship of temporal responsibilities within a nation to the broader spiritual responsibilities on membership in the universal church.[40]

As a church we continue with our role of identity transmission across borders and generations. The religious pluralism in the United States has led Christianity to not retreat from public life, but rather to become a central feature of the identity struggles of the new immigrants.[41] We need to remember that behind the numbers and rhetoric, there are human beings, all of them created in God's image. When we perceive immigrants as threats, that perception can lead us to attack and reject people who are different from the dominant culture.[42] Even in the United States, which is known as a nation of immigrants, there is a preference for immigrants who fit the image of the stereotypical white, Christian, hardworking American. Immigrants who are not perceived as similar might represent a threat to the white dominant culture. This ethnocentrism recently fueled by Donald Trump has led to the so-called build the wall movement, which sees outsiders as invaders visibly different to them.[43]

One of the latest research projects from Pew Research Center shows that Republicans and Democrats contrast over the most vital urgencies for the nation's immigration system. Republicans assign particular importance to border security and deportations of immigrants who are in the country illegally. Democrats place notable importance on paths to legal status for those who entered the country illegally, especially those who entered as children. About 79 percent of Republicans say that increasing deportations of immigrants residing illegally in the country is important, with nearly 49 percent calling it very important. By contrast, 39 percent of Democrats view increasing deportations as very or somewhat important, including just 12 percent who see it as very important. Conservative Republicans are the most likely to express strong support for more restrictive immigration goals such as increased border security and increased deportations. Liberal Democrats are the most supportive of creating a way for undocumented immigrants to stay in the country legally; 85 percent say this should be a central goal, including 44 percent who say it should be very important.[44]

Unfortunately, the issue of immigration, at least for the last twenty years, has not been a priority for any of the political parties. It has been used as a tool to win votes in political campaigns or promote the rejection of immigrant communities. Meanwhile, new waves of migrants continue to arrive in the United States. The American dream continues to attract migrants from all over the world, to such an extent that Latin America has become the number one route to reach the United States. Faced with this reality, the church needs to begin to depoliticize the migration issue and focus on the creation of new ecclesiological models to help those affected by the immigration journey. The issue of immigration is an invitation for the American church to look at the displaced as an opportunity to do missionary work that was previously done in other countries. Amid this entire migratory spectrum, undocumented immigrants are the most vulnerable due to their *illegal* status. Unfortunately, the daily or weekly services and church activities that take place in our gatherings, do not have the dynamics that allow us to address the different needs of this community.

CHRISTIANITY AMONG HISPANIC IMMIGRANTS

There is another aspect of immigration that, as a church, we must consider. In 2012, statistics showed that most undocumented immigrants coming from Latin America and the Caribbean embraced Christianity. At that time, Christians remained by far the largest religious group among both documented and undocumented immigrants. Over the past two decades, the United States has admitted an estimated 12.7 million Christian immigrants. There were approximately 11.1 million undocumented immigrants living in the United States in 2011. Out of that number, an estimated 9.2 million or 83 percent were Christians, most of them from Latin America.[45]

Christianity has grown in Latin America, Africa, and Asia since 1965; its growth in those areas means they now represent 60 percent of the world's Christians. There were several factors that helped the growth of Christianity in the Global South. In the Latin American context, the Roman Catholic tradition has been present since the conquest of the Americas. The supportive position of Catholicism toward the migratory phenomenon has been fundamental for the progress of Christianity in Latin America. This ecumenical posture has helped both Protestants and Catholics work together for the good *de nuestra gente*.[46] The second Vatican Council published several documents that refashioned the Church's mission. Vatican II specifically acknowledged that all Christians are people of God and asserted that the Holy Spirit is present in all Christian churches.

In addition, theological reflection in Latin America has been incredibly active. In 1979, a meeting of Latin American bishops in Puebla, Mexico developed the concept of a preferential action for the poor. Historical critiques looking back to the beginning of Spanish imperialism produced theological interpretations that shaped the evolution of the Latin American liberation theology. Gustavo Gutierrez, the pioneer of this theological movement, argued for the need for further conversion of the Catholic Church along those lines.[47] All this theological reflection on the social realities of the Latin American people has maintained the relevance of Christianity for Hispanic immigrants. The idea of a God who walks with the poor is part of the spiritual formation of many Latin American immigrants.

The American continent has been the land that has known Christianity through both traditions: Catholicism that began with the Spanish conquest in Mexico and Central and South America, and the Protestant tradition that arrived with the Anglo-American expansion through *manifest destiny*. This new wave of immigrants comes from a religious context where they live *con el Jesús en la boca*, where the name of God is held in a certain reverence either out of fear or tradition. The name of God is present in their culture.

As of 2022, 43 percent of Hispanic adults identify as Catholic, down from 67 percent in 2010. Protestants are the second largest faith group after Catholics, accounting for 21 percent of Hispanic adults, a share that has been relatively stable since 2010. Throughout these last years, Hispanic Protestants consistently have been more likely to identify as evangelical or born again.[48] This new wave of Christian immigrants not only carried our brothers and sisters who were Christians before they came to the United States, but also many converts who came to faith after their immigration journey.[49]

Worldwide, Christianity prevails as the world's largest religion, with approximately 2.2 billion adherents. Christianity has expanded around the world and the constant waves of migration in different geographical points allow the gospel to advance with incredible force. In this, the United States is not the exception. Christianity is the most evenly dispersed religion throughout the globe. Roughly equal numbers of Christians adherents live in Europe, approximately 26 percent; Latin America and the Caribbean, approximately 24 percent, and sub-Saharan Africa, about 24 percent.[50]

In 2020, there were approximately 281 million international migrants in the world. This equates to 3.6 percent of the global population. For 59 million international migrants, or 20.9 percent, Northern America was and still is the destination. Migration corridors represent an accumulation of migratory movements over time and provide a snapshot of how migration patterns have evolved into significant foreign-born populations in specific destination countries. The Mexico to United States corridor is the largest in the world, with nearly 300 million people crossing the it yearly. Recent years have also seen major migration and displacement events that have caused great hardship and trauma, as well as loss of life. In addition, there have been the displacements of millions of people due to conflict, or severe economic and political instability. There have also been large-scale displacements triggered by climate- and weather-related disasters in many parts of the world since 2020 and 2021.[51]

As of 2017, the immigrant population in the United States is generally accepted to be approximately 44.4 million, composing 13.6 percent of the population. US-born children of immigrants compose an additional 12 percent of the population. Projections estimate the number of immigrants to grow to 19 percent of the total population by 2050.[52] There are about 11 million undocumented immigrants living across the United States. These undocumented immigrants represent a loss of control over national identity and are seen as a threat to America being overtaken by un-American people.[53] In 2019, 44.9 million immigrants comprised 14 percent of the national population. The United States was home to 22.0 million women, 20.4 million men, and 2.5 million children who were immigrants. The top countries of origin for immigrants were Mexico with 24 percent of immigrants, India with 6 percent, China with 5 percent, the Philippines with 4.5 percent, and El Salvador with 3 percent. In 2019, 38.3 million people in the United States—that is, 12 percent of the country's population—were native-born Americans who had at least one immigrant parent.[54]

According to the Pew Research Center, monthly encounters between US Border Patrol agents and immigrants trying to cross into the country at the US-Mexico border remain at stages not seen in more than two decades. In 2020, immigrants from Mexico and the Northern Triangle countries of El Salvador, Guatemala, and Honduras were reported to be the majority of those encountered at the border. Nonetheless, by November 2022, 63 percent of the immigrants encountered at the border were from countries other than Mexico and the Northern Triangle region. Newer increases have included people from Colombia, Cuba, Nicaragua, Peru, and Venezuela. In April 2020, there were only four encounters with immigrants from Colombia, but by November 2022, that number increased to 15,439. In April 2020, there were 161 encounters with immigrants from Cuba, but by November 2022, that number increased to 34,639. The number of immigrants from Nicaragua went from 86 to 34,162. Encounters involving people from Peru increased from 18 in April 2020 to 8,495 in November 2022. In November 2022, 143,908 encounters involved single adults, while 49,520 involved families and 12,811 involved unaccompanied minors. Seventy percent of encounters in November 2022 involved single adults, while 24 percent involved families and 6 percent of unaccompanied minors. However, the percentage of encounters involving families rose abruptly during the pandemic.[55]

Most recently, there has been a considerable increase in migrants coming from South America and crossing the Darien Gap.[56] In 2023, the total number of migrants crossing the gap reached more than 500,000. This route is just one of the many used by the constant waves of migrants seeking asylum at the United States border.[57] In addition, we have waves of caravans mainly coming from Central America hoping for an opportunity to enter the country.

The reality is that the arrival of new immigrants will not stop, and the expectation that the United States will continue to experience large flows of immigrants in the near future requires us to rethink the way we do church. Furthermore, the fact that a massive number of these new pilgrims are our brothers and sisters in Christ, therefore, part of the church, makes the reflection of what God has for the future of the American church through the immigration phenomenon much more fascinating.

WAVES OF REVIVAL: NEED FOR PASTORAL CARE

The interaction between politics and the immigration issue has only resulted in fruitless discourse for at least the last two decades. *Red* and *Blue* politics have only used immigration, on the one hand, to deliver unfulfilled promises, and on the other, to promote a negative image of the immigrant community. The attitude of politics toward this social reality does not help our mission as a church at all. In addition, the most common nationalist discourse regarding this issue, and somewhat negative description of our times, shows immigration as a national crisis. Metaphors have been used to represent this phenomenon, in a derogatory manner, as a *rising tide* or a *flood* that is going to deluge the United States and swamp American society with unwanted foreigners. These metaphors also allude to war imagery, representing it as an *invasion* in which the border patrol agents seek to contain the line in a vain attempt to defend the border against the attacks of foreign invaders who carry out suicide attacks.

This also does not promote the values of a conciliatory God, much less the catholicity of the church.

The dynamics between the American church and immigration policy have been marked by constant and progressive engagement. However, these dynamics do not diminish the enormous pastoral work that lies ahead of us. Its magnitude is so great that it cannot be ignored. This reality raises countless complex situations that present sudden and unexpected challenges. Every day, the pastor in the margins interacts with a large number of people who reflect and remind them of their own condition, as well as the conflicts and difficulties other immigrant face. Such experiences can be exhausting, emotionally demanding, and spiritually debilitating, due to identification or over-identification with the people we serve.

The demand for pastoral work on the margins, or in this case, with the immigrant community, exceeds the norms of an already, by nature, very demanding function. Pastoral work involves various integral aspects of formation, restoration, and equipping. These are aspects that cover all facets of life, not only individually, but also as a community of faith. For pastoral work to achieve the healthy development of an immigrant Christian, especially in the first generation, it is necessary to create activities and provide not only spiritual resources, but also psychological and educational experiences that facilitate adaptation to the new culture and support immigrants in their establishment process in the United States. Consequently, there is a need for more pastors to care and empower the new wave of Christians arriving, whether documented or undocumented. The way they arrive in the country does not take away from the needs of this community. Therefore, the immigration phenomenon as such represents a two-dimensional challenge for the American church: (1) *The need to create new ecclesiological models to better minister to this vulnerable community,* and (2) *The increase in the demands of pastoral work because of the vast and complex needs among the immigrant community.*

CHAPTER ONE

Defining the Immigrant Community

To fully understand Hispanics in the United States today, we need to understand their unique, complex, and evolving religious traditions and ethnic identity. The Americas before its conquest by the Spaniards and its evangelization by Catholic missionaries, was a great mosaic of more or less polytheistic religions, including those of the Aztec, Inca, Mayan, Guaraní, and Mapuche. Various mythologies show us their conceptions of the world, of humanity, and of the gods. For the most part these great mythologies are known in abundant detail thanks, above all, to the stories of the first missionaries in the Americas. Unfortunately, it is often lamented today in certain intellectual, political, and even religious circles that the Spanish missionaries and conquerors did not respect the beliefs of the Indigenous cultures, and they destroyed everything in the name of God.

Commentators and scholars have studied why the conquerors acted so ruthlessly in *el nuevo mundo*. John F. Schwaller argues that there were different phases of this conquest or cultural contact. The Spanish moved first from an approach based on their own assumptions and misconceptions of the Indigenous cultures to a deeper understanding and appreciation of the cultural difference. Both Spaniards and the Indigenous peoples became more skilled in interpreting the actions and intentions of the other.[1] This cultural contact came through military power, logically motivated by economic interests, and once the conquest was perpetuated, the religion, language, and all the cultural baggage of the conquerors prevailed.[2]

In fact, there will always be a debate about that historical moment, but the reality is that we cannot change the result; we are, all of us, the result of that conquest and evangelization, or cultural contact. Consequently, Hispanic religious traditions owe their origins to the encounter between Iberian Catholicism and Indigenous people, but also to African strains. More than 4 million enslaved Africans were transported to Brazil and more than 2 million were sent to Spanish America.[3] Beginning in the sixteenth century and for centuries after, Spanish, Portuguese, French, and Dutch traders systematically acquired considerable numbers of African slaves. Africans tended to supplement and combine elements of their own religions with that of the colonizers. For example, a common belief in African societies was the conviction of a supreme creator ruler of the cosmos, who was not involved in the daily affairs of humans.[4] Based on the first commandment, Christianity demanded exclusivity. However, Africans tended to combine elements of their own religions with the new religion proposed or imposed by the colonizers.

In our context, perhaps the most well-known religious symbol for Hispanics in the United States is *La Morenita* of Guadalupe. According to legend, the Virgin of Guadalupe appeared to Juan Diego near Tepeyac, a mountain on the northwestern outskirts of Mexico City. The dark skin of the virgin contrasted with the images of white-skinned virgins brought by the *conquistadores*. This power of hope offered by the appearance of *La Morenita* was received as confirmation of the presence of God in the midst of the Indigenous people who had been outraged, and the mestizo people born illegitimately and orphaned. With *La Morenita*, the illegitimate and orphaned people found their mother; perhaps, that is why the Virgin of Guadalupe is known as the mother of Mexico.[5]

In general, Latin America is a diverse mosaic of different ways of embracing and accommodating conquest Christianity to local practices. Scholars frequently describe these practices as a syncretic blend of Indigenous and European elements.[6] Hispanics arise from a violent mix between European and Amerindian people. The knowledge of God was imposed, and with imposition came tradition, and tradition has truncated the path for us to discover or express true spirituality.

José Vasconcelos, a Latin American philosopher, reflected on the origin and purpose of the Americas in his book *The Cosmic Race*, writing about the emergence of a new race in the Americas: the fifth race, the cosmic race. Vasconcelos points out that America is the place where all races reside, and because of that, acquiring treasure from all previous races, a new race will emerge.[7] For Virgilio Elizondo, the Catholic conquest of the Americas brought with it a new people, a new ethnos, *la raza mestiza*.[8] To define the Hispanic in the United States is to contemplate someone who is in search of being. They are the ones who reveal themselves to the imposition of misfortune and religious chimeras to go in search of emancipation from orphanhood and limitations and show their full potential.

TWO WAVES, TWO TRADITIONS

The first European migration to America began with what is commonly known as the conquest or discovery of America. During the first wave of Christian immigrants in the Roman Catholic tradition, the main protagonists of the first evangelization in America were the Franciscans, Dominicans, Augustinians, and Mercedarians. In the second half of the sixteenth century the Jesuits joined. In 1567, they founded schools in Lima, Cuzco, and Potosí, a prelude to what would be their teaching and missionary activity. This first wave of evangelization covered practically all the South American continent.

The second wave of Protestant traditions took place with the arrival of more European immigrants, in a combination of flight from persecution and of missionary zeal. This second wave came with the settlements of colonists in 1607 and in 1620. The longing for greater economic opportunity, together with the desire for religious freedom, impelled these first immigrants to leave their homes. By

1630 Puritans migrated to New England. Meanwhile, Maryland was home for English Catholics. The Quakers founded Pennsylvania in 1681, but they had previously established settlements in West New Jersey. The longing of each continuous displaced wave for its right to practice its religion facilitated freedom of worship, which became a central part of the American creed:[9] "The Protestant colonizers saw themselves engaged in a divine enterprise."[10] The doctrine of manifest destiny justified the great western expansion.

Protestant expansionism collided with the Catholic colonial empire as American settlers started to move into the northern regions of what was Mexican territory. There was also a clear feeling of religious competition between Protestants and Catholics. Battles, wars, and other conflicts often had a religious nuance. Citizens in each country saw their encounter with the other as a chance to demonstrate that their faith expression was more correct. Their expansions were often interpreted as proof of the superiority of their religious expression. Even today, at soccer games, advertisements sometimes allude to the battles these two nations have had and transfer them to the soccer field.[11]

In 1848, under the Treaty of Guadalupe-Hidalgo, Mexico ceded to the United States a vast territory, approximately half the size of the prewar Mexico.[12] This treaty created a geographic border but did not limit or stop the continuation of the mixture of the two theological traditions.

After the United States conquered northern Mexico, armed resistance erupted in various places. In other instances, Spanish-speaking residents defended their rights in the political arena. They were strangers in their own land. These religious traditions, Catholic and Protestant, provided an ongoing means of public communal expression and affirmation. Such interaction enabled the two traditions to overcome pluralistic ignorance and become aware of other distinct traditions than theirs.[13] It is important to highlight that for Hispanics there is a very marked difference between Catholics and Protestants; in many places in Mexico and Latin America there is still a rejection of Protestant Christianity.

In some cases, Protestant Christianity is even perceived as a threat and is banned.

Historically, each wave of the different branches of Christianity, large or small, has given a different nuance to the American church. European migrants and local migrants have created a unique America. Migration waves have shaped the history of the United States, and they continue to orchestrate tremendous changes in US social and cultural institutions as well as religious organizations.[14] Oscar Handlin once said, "Once I thought to write a history of the immigrants in America. Then I discovered that the immigrants were American history."[15] Most immigrants shared two hopes: a better life and economic opportunity. These hopes contributed greatly to developing a spirit of personal betterment in American society and to strengthening national confidence in change and the future.[16]

The two theological traditions that shaped the religious spectrum of the American continent are present in this internal wave of Hispanics coming to the United States. The wave of Hispanic immigrants in the past decades has been the one that has had the most impact on the country as it has spread wider geographically in the country. Like many of the first pilgrims who settled in this nation, what the Hispanic displaced have in common is the Christian faith. "Even the most conservative extrapolation suggests that, in the last half a century, more than 30 million Christians have been added . . . by immigration alone"[17] to the American church. With this influx of newly displaced Hispanic Christians, Christianity in the United States will take a new direction with new nuances and features.

PORTRAYALS OF HISPANICS IN THE UNITED STATES

Anybody who wishes to minister among Hispanics in the United States should recognize that they are not all alike; they are, in fact, a diverse group of people. We might seem to be all the same to the untrained eye, but in reality, we are a very complex mixture of races.[18] Therefore, it is important to highlight that the term *Hispanic* generalizes the different nationalities of Mexico, the Caribbean, Central America, South America, and Spain. The term *Hispanic* is also applied to Puerto Ricans, who are born citizens of the United States. Also, Brazilians are not considered Hispanic because they speak Portuguese, but they are part of South America. This term was first used in 1970 and is not based on ethnicity, race, geography, or nationality. Different entities or agencies in the United States classify Hispanics as Americans who identify themselves as being of a Spanish-speaking background.[19] There have been many debates about the use of this term to identify Hispanics in the United States. These debates are just a reflection of the complexity of being considered Latino, Latina, Latinx, or Hispanic. The nationality of each Hispanic group affects their immigration experience because the US immigration policy benefits each group in different ways.

One of the groups of Hispanics that benefits from the diverse US Immigration policies is the residents of *La Isla del Encanto*. Puerto Rico has the right, granted by the United States, to elect its governor and to have jurisdiction over certain matters of local administration, reserving the rights to immigration and military issues, among others. Puerto Ricans are born as American citizens and have the same rights. They are the second largest population of Hispanic origin living in the United States. Unlike some other Caribbean countries, Puerto Ricans are not exposed to the risks or suffering of the pursuit of the American dream.

Cubans, like Puerto Ricans, have a different immigration experience than the average Hispanic immigrant. The policy known as the *wet/dry feet law* shows how they benefit. After the ninety-mile journey by sea, the moment they set foot on US territory they become objects of acquired rights and cannot be deported. The difference is that Cubans are fleeing political oppression, while other groups of Hispanics are fleeing economic oppression or government corruption. Cubans have an impressive influence in Miami. Many of them are powerful magnates with political influence.[20]

Temporary protected status (TPS) was established by the US government in 1990. This program allows migrants whose home countries are considered unsafe the right to live and work in the United States. Many Central Americans have remained in the United States with temporary protected status. Though they are not considered lawful permanent residents or US citizens, this program has allowed them to live freely in the United States for more than thirty years. In addition, many of them have benefited from family reunification channels and obtained a lawful permanent US residency. As of 2019, approximately 2.1 million unauthorized immigrants from Central America were living in the United States. Most of these Central Americans had limited English proficiency.[21]

South Americans first started immigrating to the United States during the Cold War era, when countries such Argentina, Chile, and Colombia experienced political turmoil, armed conflict, and economic instability. Since then, immigration from that part of the Americas has continued to be driven by a mix of those same reasons. Recently, we have witnessed a massive influx of Venezuelans since conditions in their country have worsened under Nicolás Maduro's political regime. South Americans in the United States tend to have higher educational skills than other Hispanic groups. Usually, most of them obtain lawful permanent residence in the United States through family connections. Others are more likely to obtain a green card via a refugee or asylum pathway.[22] I currently pastor three Colombian families who are in this process; one of them will likely receive their work permit before this book is published.

Recently, encounters of South Americans arriving without authorization at the US-Mexican border have increased dramatically. Currently, more than one million of the estimated unauthorized immigrants in the United States are from South America. Another important aspect to consider is the fact that the physical features of many South Americans are very similar to Caucasians; therefore, they tend to suffer less racism or rejection.[23] It is important not to lose sight of what is known as the Darien Gap. This migration route is an unrestrained wilderness region on the border of Colombia and Panama, crowded with everything from deadly snakes to antigovernment guerrillas. The region witnesses a monumental flow of migrants from Cuba, Africa, and Asia, whose desperation leads them on a dangerous journey to the American dream.

Historically, Mexicans are the largest group of Hispanics in the United States. The main reason for this is the annexation of Mexican territory as part of the United States mentioned earlier. Literally, the border crossed them. Additionally, we are neighbors. This closeness makes it very tempting for Mexicans to come to the United States. Currently, they comprise almost 60 percent of the Hispanic population in United States. From 2000 to 2021, the number of people of Mexican origin living in the United States increased by 79 percent, growing from 20.9 million to 37.2 million. The Mexican foreign-born population in the United States has increased 23 percent, from 8.7 million in 2000 to 10.7 million in 2021. Thirty-five percent of foreign-born Mexicans are US citizens. The Mexican population in the United Stated is mainly concentrated in California, Texas, Arizona, Illinois, and Colorado.[24] In addition, out of the approximately 11 million undocumented immigrants in the country, approximately 5.3 million—almost 48 percent—are Mexicans.[25]

As of 2020, the Hispanic population reached 62.1 million, an increase of 11.6 million since the 2010 Census.[26] The cultural variety within each group of Hispanics is incredible, and worthy of an in-depth study in order to understand each nation. However, for practical reasons and to present a portrait of Hispanics in the United States, it is best to classify them into five main regional groups:

Mexican (57.7% of the Hispanic population)
Caribbean (16.2%)
Central American (9.5%)
South American (6.5%)
Other, Hispanic or Spanish (10.5%)

FIRST GENERATION PROFILE

Due to the complexity of the immigration journey and the diversity of cases, we cannot create absolutes regarding the profile of the immigrant. However, there are certain characteristics that we can highlight to better understand this community. The first generation of Hispanic immigrants who come to the United States, for the most part, do so because they do not have enough resources in their homeland. Most Hispanics come from the most desperate and deprived areas in Latin America.[27] We come with a huge desire to have a better life. Many of us did not have the opportunity to have an adequate education for two basic reasons: because we did not have the resources, and because we were not raised in families that promoted education. Overall, 27 percent of recent Hispanic immigrants to the United States aged twenty-five and older have earned at least a bachelor's degree in the United States or elsewhere, up from 11 percent in 2000, but almost 75 percent have no experience in college education.[28]

In assessing their social values, first-generation immigrants are likely to express views generally considered more conservative than second-generation immigrants. When asked whether they thought divorce was unacceptable, nearly half (46 percent) of first-generation immigrants reported they believe it is unacceptable. When asked about abortion, more than eight in ten (83 percent) said it is unacceptable. In their attitudes toward their future, 53 percent of first-generation immigrants agree that "it doesn't do any good to plan for the future because you don't have any control over it."

Attitudes toward immigration are also considerably different by generation. When asked in 2002 whether the United States should allow more, allow the same, or reduce the number of immigrants working in this country legally, 52 percent of first-generation immigrants thought the United States should allow more immigrants to work here legally. Attitudes toward undocumented immigration were even more pronounced. When asked whether undocumented immigrants help or hurt the economy, eight in ten (81 percent) of first-generation migrants reported undocumented immigrants help the economy. Furthermore, the overwhelming majority (91 percent) of first-generation immigrants report agreeing that it is better for children to live in their parents' home until they get married. Likewise, an overwhelming majority of first-generation migrants (92 percent) believe that relatives are more important than friends.[29]

This profile changes, however, with the second and third generations of Hispanics in the United States. This is due to a variation in the way they identify themselves. For example, in a 2019 survey, 22 percent of the second generation identify themselves as American, and 33 percent of the third generation do the same. Only 20 percent of the third generation speaks Spanish and 44 percent of the second. Thirteen percent of the third generation socialize with Hispanics, while 28 percent of the second generation do so. Fifteen percent of the third generation celebrate Hispanic cultural celebrations and 23 percent of the second generation. Thirteen percent in both generations identify as Catholic. In general, a very low percentage of the second and third generation feels connected to what is happening to other Hispanics. Only 10 percent of the third generation and 20 percent of the second generation said that what happens to other Hispanics impacts their life a lot.[30]

Another subject that is important to the first-generation immigrants is health care. More than half of adult undocumented immigrants (59%) had no health insurance during all of 2007.[31] For the undocumented immigrant, a basic physical check-up is not feasible, much less is attending to some discomfort in their body. They look for other ways to alleviate their discomfort, be it ordering medicine from Tijuana, looking for a *sobador*,[32] using home remedies, or other non-traditional resources. An important aspect to highlight is that the first generation tends to resist being treated by a doctor. In Mexico they call doctors *matasanos* (quack doctors); there is a tendency in our minds that doctors do not help cure diseases or that they do not help with treatment. In some Hispanic religious circles, there is even a rejection of medical care; in these circles, faith in God must be absolute to be healed and there is no need to go to the doctor. In fact, my grandfather in Mexico died for not being treated by a doctor, as he was waiting to be healed by God.

Another very common aspect in families with undocumented parents is the limitations that affect how they raise their children. A third of the children of undocumented immigrants and a fifth of adult undocumented immigrants live in poverty. There is a very heavy financial burden on most undocumented immigrants and this brings many problems, because settling in this country will always require a stable financial situation. Due to the lack of financial resources, undocumented families must share housing or live in very small spaces. Their budgets are very limited, and their priorities are based on paying their rent, their food, and their utilities. Some also feel a responsibility to help their families back in their home countries. Some of the families I currently pastor are still paying off the money they had to borrow to get to this country. An analysis of college attendance finds that among undocumented immigrants aged eighteen to twenty-four who have graduated from high school, half (49%) are in college or have attended college. Adult undocumented immigrants are disproportionately likely to be poorly educated. Among undocumented immigrants aged twenty-five to sixty-four, 47 percent have less than a high school education.[33] Due to the need to provide for their families, parents spend time working, and this affects their interaction with their children and their involvement with their education. In addition, the lack of familiarity with the educational system, the language barriers, and the need to improve their financial situation means many families motivate their children to find a job and not to study.

A PICTURE OF THE SPANISH LANGUAGE

El idioma del Cielo (the language of heaven) is a phrase a professor used to say at Fuller when referring to the Spanish language.[34] A few decades ago, the sentiment "this is America, we speak English" was a much more common opinion toward foreign languages. Today in America there is an openness and willingness to engage Spanish and other languages. When it comes to the salvation of millions of souls, we should have a more self-sacrificing attitude toward Spanish.[35] The American church is learning to speak Spanish.

Obviously, Spanish is the language spoken by all Hispanics, but it is important to observe that there are expressions, accents, and other peculiar linguistic aspects to each Hispanic nationality. Cervantes's language was consolidated with *Don Quixote de la Mancha*. However, there are still places in Latin America where dialects that survived the conquest are spoken. Among others we find Quechua, Guarani, Nahuatl, Aymara, and Mapudungun. However, Spanish, literally, is the language that identifies Hispanics.

Various pronunciations create sounds very different from one country to another. It is a distinctive experience to listen to somebody with the accent and intonation of an Argentinian versus a Mexican. The Spanish of Central America is also different from that of Chile or Peru. I personally love the Colombian accent. Variations in accents, tones, words: the differences are more evident for people who are native Spanish speakers or have a high level of knowledge of the Spanish language. There are plenty of expressions that vary depending on the region. For example: a bus is called *colectivo* in Argentina and *autobús* in Mexico. A waiter is called *mesero* in Mexico and *mozo* in Peru. Work is called *trabajo* in Mexico and *pega* in Chile. The list goes on and on.

In countries like Argentina and Uruguay, they use *vos* to address a person, while in the rest of Latin America *tu* is mainly used. The reason for this is that when the Spanish arrived in America in the fifteenth century, *vos* was the more common pronoun, and it has remained so in those two countries until today. The Reina Valera version of the Bible has contributed to the retention of the use of these pronouns; instead of *ustedes*, *vosotros* is used.

Another interesting phenomenon concerning language has to do with what is known as Spanglish. Bilingual native speakers of English and Spanish, or individuals in the process of learning the language, often present cases of phonetic fusion or subdifferentiation, whereby a phonological contrast in one of the systems disappears in contact with the other system. In most cases, lexical transfer includes phonological and morphological adaptations that facilitate its insertion into the Spanish grammatical system. Thus, words like *troca* from truck, *carpeta* from carpet, *fulear* from full, *marketa* from market, *parkiar* from parking, and so on, are incorporated into Spanish having been inserted into the inflectional morphological paradigm of the language.³⁶ The mixture of English and Spanish presents some surprising results.³⁷

The continual waves of Hispanic migrants to the United States have kept Spanish a vibrant language in this country for many years. The role of Spanish in the United States is also linked to the future of Puerto Rico. The Spanish language has a legal status in the United States, though only on the island of Puerto Rico. But with the arrival of new waves, Spanish becomes a language that causes curiosity and desire to discover and learn its different variants among different nationalities.³⁸

FACES MARKED BY SOCIAL ABSENCE

I mentioned in the introduction that family life for Hispanics is very important; all members play a key role, not just the central household members. Family supersedes church, political parties, or any other group. Hispanics think and act as a family unit.³⁹ Family ties become the institution that provides the basis for the social life of the individual. Therefore, family detachment leaves the displaced practically in social limbo. It is important for us to understand and keep in mind that the social life of those who decide to leave their homeland is deeply affected. Not only do they break with many of the relationships established in the familiarity of their native community, but also, now in the United States, they enter a multicultural place. Multiculturalism can be difficult for the displaced to assimilate, especially if they come from rural areas. Exposure to the fast-paced world of the city, and lack of familiarity with everything, discourages rebuilding a new social life.

Although most immigrants integrate into Hispanic communities already established in the United States, in their daily lives they also must coexist with other cultures. Their social life often fails to flourish or enrich itself with the assimilation of the existence of other cultures. So, the immigrant lives a socially absent life. Multicultural societies often have access to a wider range of international experiences. However, challenges can include communication barriers, misunderstandings, and occasional tensions between different cultural groups. Cultural clashes can occur, and it can be difficult to maintain a shared national identity. The sense of community and connection with people can be fleeting or almost non-existent. The immigrant is socially absent due to the loss of social connections left behind in their homeland, but also because they are unable to connect with or assimilate other cultures.[40] Juan Francisco Martinez defines this group of Hispanic as "nuclear," people who live almost completely within the Hispanic community and have limited contact with the new culture. They only speak Spanish and proudly protect every aspect of their culture.[41]

In addition, immigrants' social circles are often defined by social divisions of labor. They are often ignored and not recognized as contributing members of society. The displaced usually perform menial jobs that are poorly compensated, perceived as unworthy or with a lack of dignity. Having this type of job causes us to be perceived as a community with a lack of ambition, lack of skills, and lack of creativity and imagination.[42]

The social absence of the displaced arises from the fragmentation in their previously established relationships and the challenge of multiculturalism. They live a fragmented, incomplete social life, with relationships on hold due to distance, while struggling to establish new ones in a diverse community. Hispanics are very emotional; we are people of the heart. We are more emotional than rational, more feelings than logic. A truth said only with logic and without heart or emotion will not be well received.[43]

For some migrants, this social absence is because in their countries of origin their lifestyle was in professional circles. They are educated people with academic degrees, but now, due to their condition, they must work in factories, hotels, restaurants, or in the fields. Currently, I pastor several people who suffer constant attacks of despair because they cannot obtain the same lifestyle they had back in their countries. They get frustrated, angry, and are not happy with the job they have, because it is not something they are passionate about. The need to generate income has them there, and their condition forces them to stay in that workplace.

SCARS OF POLITICAL ABSENCE

The political formation of Hispanics is familiarly associated with political scandals, fraud, and corruption. Unfortunately, that is the image in many of us when we talk about Latin American politics. In fact, many of the new waves of immigrants are the product of political oppression. Latin American people do not expect to have a good president. Political disillusion has generated distrust in the political entities of our countries. The phrase "all politicians are the same" is born from the great disappointments suffered through the ages in Latin America.

When the Hispanic migrant arrives in the United States, their political life is already marked by disillusionment, and therefore political separation. Here in the United States, they understand that because of their status as foreigners their political point of view will not be heard. Their political opinions are not valid because they do not have the privilege of voting. If the immigrants somehow manage to fix their immigration status, the process to be able to actively vote is very slow. They cannot vote if they have a work permit or a residence card; they need to wait to become a citizen of the United States. As Hispanics, political powerlessness remains a significant cause of the oppression we experience as a community. At present we have some influence in state politics and within our local communities, but minimal representation, political voice, or influence to determine or create significant changes at the national level.[44]

The displaced live in a political limbo. We are aware not only of what is happening in the United States, but also our countries of origin, all without being able to exercise a full political life. For the majority of those who manage to become American citizens, their political life is limited to the act of obeying the laws, but we do not participate in the formulation of new ones.

GESTURES OF CULTURAL DILEMMA

Some years ago, a seminary professor of mine, in reference to the exiled Jews in Babylon, said that, for the exiled, the text (the Old Testament) was the motherland. When the displaced person is far from their homeland, they adhere to anything that reminds them of their culture. They hold on, not putting their cultural identity at risk, even though everyone who lives in the United States must adapt to majority culture at some level. Most likely the individual will look for ways to maintain a particular identity. Often, recent immigrants or older adults primarily live within their communities and have limited contact with the majority culture.[45] They may even perceive the new culture as a threat.

This cultural mourning generates in the displaced a tendency to hang on to objects from the world they left behind. Religious symbols and food become important. Every image, flavor, or color from their country of origin becomes sacred. The feelings and emotions experienced by the longing for your land are indescribable.[46] Personally, one of the psalms that has helped me to mitigate the longing for my homeland is Psalm 137. This psalm arises from the melancholy of losing your country, your land, and your flag. It is the cry of the soul that breaks the thresholds of the eyes and overflows to touch your heart. It is an infinite, inexhaustible cry. The routine of life normalizes it, but just one sigh is enough for the tears to rush once again, flooding the depths of your being. This psalm is the infinite sadness of not being able to set foot on your land, of not being able to look at its sunsets or its sunrises. It is not being able to enjoy its aroma. It is living off memories. It is impotence that prevails. It is the deafening scream of reality that screams in your face that you are far from your loved ones. It is the voice of silence that whispers hope, the hope of returning to your land. It is the pact from a distance that promises not to forget the sky where you were born, nor the streets that smiled when you ran in them. It is the claim in prayer to your God who continues to be with you. It is blaming the events that took you away from home. It is living with the longing to return to the dust from which you were formed and become part of its land once buried.

Although I have mentioned that there are notable differences among each group of Hispanics, there are some characteristics in common. Some colonial Spanish values have transcended the independence of Hispanic nations and have remained part of the cultural identity of this community. Hispanics tend to be conservative or traditional in their lifestyle and culture. The machismo in Hispanic men clearly separates them from American men. Hispanic women also have a very different role from American women. These traits are especially evident in recent immigrants. *Machismo* refers to the manliness expected of the man, who must be physically strong, not afraid, and an authoritative figure in the family, with the obligation to protect and provide for his family. In many Hispanic contexts a *real man* is one who has his wife and children in complete subjection. He is the ruler and governs with an iron fist. He likes to drink and believes himself to be a *Latin lover*, a *Don Juan*.[47] The complementary role of women is *Marianism*, which refers to a self-sacrificing, religious woman, responsible for the chores of the home and the training and care of children. The religious life is dominated by women; they are the religious stalwarts of the family.[48] Motherhood is a very important goal for women in Hispanic culture, and as mothers they are expected to sacrifice themselves for their children and take care of elderly relatives. Although acculturation and the need for Hispanic women to work have changed their roles a little, in general these roles still exist. It is also worth noting that Hispanic single moms are the second largest group of single moms in the United States.

PORTRAYALS OF HISPANIC CHURCHES

After 1960 the Hispanic community became more ethnically diverse in the United States. These new immigrants took on important leadership roles in denominations and strongly shaped the face of the Hispanic Church throughout the twenty-first century. From 1960 until the present day most of the growth reported by existing denominations and emerging movements can be directly connected to the growth of the Hispanics and to the increasing impact of Protestantism, both among the Spanish-speaking population in the United States and throughout Latin America. It is the evangelical and Pentecostal groups that are growing, often quite quickly. And it is the historic denominations, some of which had a longer history among Hispanics, that are either not growing or are finding it difficult to expand their movements among this community. Today the revival caused by what Joseph Castleberry calls the *new pilgrims* is clearly visible.[49]

Today, in a nationwide phenomenon, some churches have opted to launch new ministries focused on these new pilgrims. In particular, "Protestant Evangelical and Pentecostal congregations are increasingly drawing Latino immigrants to their more emotionally expressive and interactive worship services."[50] Some theologians have concluded that, "the arrival of millions of new immigrants to America in our time virtually guarantees a strong future for Christianity."[51] This trend in migration does not seem likely to stop anytime soon. In the last two administrations we have witnessed a considerable increase in the arrival of new displaced people from Latin America. For many, there is a revolution of vibrant Christian immigrants shifting the course of the American church. More than two-thirds of first-generation Hispanic immigrants are Catholic. Hispanic ministries in the most popular denominations, especially Pentecostals, and many independent churches have been growing tremendously all over the United States. In those Hispanic ministries, 50 to 80 percent of members have converted since coming to the United States. The same pattern has been evident for Chinese, Filipino, African, and Caribbean migrants.[52]

These emerging churches or ministries meet in basements of historic church buildings, parks, homes, parking lots, and garages, and many of them have bought their own buildings. Many start as small congregations, then become large congregations where hundreds gather.[53] About ten years ago, I was part of one of the many churches renting the same huge old church building in Pasadena, California, on the corner of Walnut and Los Robles. We were using the basement, but there were at least two more Hispanic ministries renting other rooms in the same building. That ministry in Pasadena is part of an association of more than twenty other churches, all of them founded by first generation immigrants. In the Hispanic community, immigration is a movement where millions of migrants are our brothers and sisters in the faith. There are many others turning to faith after they arrive in the United States. All of them are part of the global church, created in God's image, and all of them are becoming part of the American church. They are changing the context of many historic, almost-abandoned church buildings, where attendance is decreasing. Immigrants and their future generations will make Christianity in America more vibrant and relevant. Christian immigrants mean to turn America back to its historic identity, to make America a shining city on a hill so that the world may see the glory of God.[54]

Another notable effect of immigration in the Hispanic context is what is occurring in the academic field. In the past two decades there has been a considerable number of Hispanics obtaining graduate degrees in theology. There are many recognized organizations for Hispanic theologians. Perhaps the most well-known is Asociación para la Educación Teológica Hispana (AETH).[55] The Hispanic Summer Program (HSP) was born out of several efforts to advance theological education and pastoral leadership among Hispanics. Another well-known institution is the Hispanic Theological Initiative (HTI). Its focus is supporting Hispanic PhD students who are committed to serving the academy and the church. It provides financial and mentorship support to these students in order to increase the number of Hispanic faculty in theological education.[56]

In regions like southern California, there are plenty of universities with a Hispanic department or program where a considerable number of Hispanic leaders pursue formal academic formation. While I was pursuing a master's degree at Azusa Pacific University, I learned that Vanguard University and Biola University now have their own Hispanic programs. At the time, I transferred to Fuller

Theological Seminary to finish my master's program. I learned that Pepperdine University has a center that embraces Liberation Theology as the foundation for its education.

The most well-known Protestant Hispanic organization today is the National Hispanic Christian Leadership Conference (NHCLC). The NHCLC is world's largest Hispanic Christian organization serving as a representative voice for the more than 100 million Hispanic Evangelicals. Also, the National Latino Evangelical Coalition (NaLEC) provides alternative voices to the existing partisan voices and to create national awareness about the growing number of Hispanic Evangelicals who are not captive to partisan politics. Esperanza is the oldest of the three national organizations, but it came into national prominence at the beginning of the twenty-first century. Esperanza came to the nation's attention in 2001 when it began to host the National Hispanic Prayer Breakfast and Conference, which is often attended by the president of the United States.[57]

The immigration of Hispanics has become relevant once again in the history of the United States in recent times, not only because of the growing number of displaced arriving at the border, but also because of polarization and divided opinions on the subject even within the church. What is important to highlight is that the Christian faith has never been lacking in each wave of new migrants, and that has caused a positive impact on the American church as such. The evidence we have today is that most of the newly displaced share our faith. So, it is important to ask ourselves, what will God do with these new pilgrims?

LETTER FROM AN UNDOCUMENTED CHRISTIAN

What does it mean to be undocumented? In my case, it meant exposing myself to very extreme and unpredictable situations because I did not have sufficient resources to process proper documentation to enter legally into this country. I migrated not necessarily because of the desire to leave my country or relatives, but because of the needs of my family and the lack of opportunities. It meant almost starving to death and getting lost somewhere in the mountains between San Diego and Tijuana. It meant taking the responsibilities of an adult while being a teenager. It meant suffering in silence all the effects of migration and not being able to ask for help for fear of being deported or being wrongly judged. It meant not being able to study or prepare as a normal teenager. I needed to learn the language in an adult school, and then wished to go to college, but I found out that classes cost much more for an international student. I always felt imprisoned for not having the freedom that a legal status provides. I experienced frustration because, according to the system, I did not exist, and there are a lot of limitations for an undocumented person. I lived an incomplete life for not being able to physically reunite with those who were left behind.

When I got married, I experienced greater anxiety. Now, I was no longer alone; first my wife, and then my son, carried the limitations of living with an undocumented person. At that time the situation was much more complex. My biggest fear was losing my mother or father in Mexico and being in the predicament of what to do, either leaving my wife alone in the United States to go to Mexico to say goodbye, but not being able to return, or experience the regret of not being able to say goodbye at their last moments. Thank God that didn't happen! Then the pandemic came, and my legal process stopped and then was prolonged. As if that was not enough, the anti-immigrant rhetoric of 2016 had further increased anxiety and fear. A few years ago, I finally had the opportunity to hug and kiss my mother after more than twenty years without being able to do so. In a hug that lasted an eternity, with groans of joy, sadness, nostalgia, forgiveness, and a mix of many intense emotions, I let my arms, and my tears, tell my mother how much it hurt me to have been away from her. I filled her with kisses and kissed her hands, asking her forgiveness for making her spend sleepless nights worrying about me.

God used that movement to a new country 24 years ago to call me to be part of his church. Honestly, being part of the church was not part of my plans. However, my migratory journey was the path that God used for me to recognize my need for Christ. Since I had that first experience with God, my love for the church emerged in an inexplicable way. I have had a passion for being involved and serving in the local church, and I have tried to do my best for the kingdom of God. Through the Bible, I have discovered the magnitude of how powerful it is to belong to a universal church. Isn't it incredible that thousands of people around the world gather to celebrate the name of Christ? That is powerful!

In these years living in the United States, I have learned to love this great nation. Let us continue praying together for this country. May the love and unity that exists between us be an example for those who have lost their faith and for the new generations who have distanced themselves from the church. Also, I want to ask you to please keep me in your prayers. As immigrants, we face many challenges trying to establish ourselves in this country. In the church we have found our identity as God's creation, God's family, and God's loved ones. Unfortunately, there have been no resolutions for immigration reform. It is not easy to live undocumented, but we trust in God and understand that our situation does not stop his purposes with his church. On the other hand, we are glad that our churches are growing greatly in this country and that many of our compatriots continue coming to Christ. We love you in Christ, and we pray that the progress of the gospel continues to make this country a light to the nations. In the love of Christ, your undocumented brother.

CHAPTER TWO

A Theology That Invites Immigrants into Belonging

In Mexico it is not strange to see houses with plaques bearing the inscription *Bienvenido, Mi Casa Es Su Casa*. Looking at that plaque hanging on the wall of a house creates a positive and warming impact on the person who visits that house. Here we might see ties to the people of Israel. In the Jewish world, the ultimate reason for hospitality lays in the nature of a loving God who opens their house to the orphan and the widow, to the poor, and the migrant, and defends them from all aggravation and injustice.

The deep feelings of anxiety, helplessness, disgrace, and disillusionment that exist in the soul of the migrant are feelings that Israel knew very well because they experienced that same sensation when they were also migrants to Egypt. From that experience, God reminds the people of Israel about the importance of making sure the stranger feels welcome.

The biblical and Jewish tradition of presenting God as the model of hospitality to all without distinction, lays the most solid foundation for our duty of understanding, welcoming, and loving. God is the Creator and Father, the great host, who welcomes us and makes us all equal. Hospitality belongs to the works of mercy whose primary model is God. These works of mercy have a special uniqueness; they not only have their reward on earth but also bring us a permanent profit in the expanding future of God's kingdom.

The notion of home is especially complex for the displaced, whose transfer or movement is entirely uncertain, impermanent, and transitory given their uncertain status in the country. Home is what they left behind, but also what they are creating in the new place, despite anxiety about the possibility of deportation. This constant fear of being deported adds a unique dimension to the transience and impermanence experienced by the individual during the process of building a sense of belonging in their new home. Home is the place where the heart is, as the phrase goes, where the roots and dreams live, where there is an umbilical cord that connects us with life. Home is not just a place; it is a feeling. The house is not only a physical place, but it is also one that is imagined, a territory—not only geographical but also a place of identity. The sense of territory may remain even when the geographic location changes, but the two senses are dynamically connected. Home's definition may change through displacement, violence, politics, and war, but identity remains connected to the place left behind. Regardless of the physical space, we strive to make a place feel like home, a place where we build a sense of belonging and where we establish community.

PROPHETIC VOICES PREPARING TO HOST

In the last decades, there have been a considerable number of theological voices addressing the displaced or exiled. Gradually, a theology about immigration emerged until we reached the moment we live in now. This reflection has not been something that has happened overnight; many men and women have literally invested their lives to be able to position the issue of immigration in a place that cannot be ignored by the American church.

These prophetic voices have brought not only a liberating perspective on immigration, but also a different narrative for this phenomenon in God's story. Virgilio Elizondo remarks that in *mestizaje* (from mestizo, mixed, hybrid), we see the end of a new era and the beginning of another. Although this concept originated at the time of the conquest by the mixture of Europeans and Indigenous or native Americans, Elizondo argues that that mixture continues to our time. This theological perspective marked the arrival or groundbreaking of Hispanic theology in the United States. Elizondo perceives immigrants living in the United States as a distinct people, a newborn ethnic strain, people wanting a better life entering the structures of opportunity, and he states that they need a North American tutoring, but they also want to retain their cultural and linguistic identity. For Elizondo, this is possible and necessary for the future of the new Americanism.[1]

In the 1990s, Justo L. Gonzalez proclaimed for Hispanics in the United States a pilgrimage to a *mañana* made possible by the death and resurrection of Jesus Christ. In his *Christian Theology from a Hispanic Perspective*, he announces the role of Hispanics in what he calls the "new reformation." For Gonzalez, this is a historical moment where the exiles in this country will start raising their voices and expressing their theological perspectives.[2] This new reformation will arise in the periphery of Christendom, in the Global South, and among minorities in the traditional centers of Christianity.

Aware of the great impact that the migratory phenomenon has historically had in the United States, it was M. Daniel Carrol R. who made the invitation for the American church to begin to reflect more consciously on the immigration issue. "If Christians want to address the problems posed by the immigration of Hispanics and contribute to possible solutions, then they should do so consciously as Christians and more specifically as biblically informed Christians."[3] Carrol reminds us about the complexities and historical dimension of immigration. Also, he reminds the American church that for those who are disciples of Christ, there are ways of looking at the migratory phenomenon that are grounded in the Bible and come from the perspective of faith.

More recently, Daniel G. Groody formulated a theology of migration that stimulates a new imagination about what it is to be a human before God. In this majestic work *A Theology of Migration*, Groody promotes unity and reconciliation. Also, he carries out a robust elaboration of what he calls "liberating narratives of migration." He exhorts us not to reduce migration to a political, economic, or social issue, but rather, to understand the movement of God through this phenomenon. His work leads us to navigate deeply in the biblical stories to understand migration from God's perspective.[4]

Another important theological approach is proposed by Cláudio Carvalhaes, who regards worship as central to the calling and to the church as a faith community. For Carvalhaes, worship inspires the community for a mission of radical social transformation. In this approach, worship becomes a subversive activity of justice in a world of injustice. The author proposes the creation of a new vocabulary for worship and prayer, one that is located amid the poor and displaced and the major issues of violence and destruction. Liturgies incorporate elements from those marginalized, displaced, or oppressed contexts.[5] Recently, I had the opportunity to participate in the development of an initiative to incorporate liturgical aspects in our worship that connect with the migratory experience. This initiative, sponsored by the Calvin Institute of Christian Worship, allowed us to reflect on the importance of the other (the displaced) in our worship. As a community of faith, we articulated that our best act of worship would be to serve the foreigner, the immigrant. Our purpose was to create awareness among church families about the catholicity of the church, pilgrimage, and movement that is expanding God's kingdom.

In June 2023, I had the opportunity to attend a conference titled "Putting a Human Face to Migration," hosted by Calvin Seminary. In one of the lectures, Leopoldo Sánchez spoke about the universal identity of the church, or "catholicity." Sánchez claims that the church can best approach the issue of immigration by talking about the church's unity in a catholic way. This concept finds its roots in the Nicene creed "I believe in the Church, that it is one, holy, catholic and apostolic." *Catholic* means universal: the church is a church that spreads throughout the whole world.[6] Within the Hispanic context, and especially in Pentecostal traditions, the word *catholic* is perceived as related to the Roman Catholic Church. There is an apathy toward everything that has to do with the Catholic Church. While I was doing my master's degree at Asuza Pacific University, I had the opportunity to interview Justo Gonzalez. I remember that in response to a question regarding liturgies in protestant churches, he told me that "as protestants, we tend to reject every element in the liturgy of the Roman Catholic Church, there is a mistrust because the word Catholic is next to the Roman word."[7] Expanding this concept of catholicity invites us to look at the church of Christ from a perspective that transcends borders.

In addition to this theological reflection regarding immigration, very prolific literature that exposes the realities and experiences of people who leave their lands in search of a better life can teach important truths. This literature has progressively increased, and it has transcended religious circles in sharing the struggles of the displaced. A recent work on this matter is *Solito* by Javier Zamora,[8] a fantastic story of an immigrant child on his mythic journey to the United States. This jewel portrays the reality of thousands of children and their families affected by the separations endured while migrating. Although the author has an incredible way of telling his story, and perhaps for a moment makes the reader forget how dangerous and heartbreaking it is for a child to get to reach the border, the book shows us the ravages and dysfunctions of the brutal migratory journey to the United States.

Another great work is *I Am Not Your Perfect Mexican Daughter* by Erika L. Sánchez.[9] The plot addresses the experience of a first-generation Mexican American struggling to reconcile two conflicting cultures. The author explores immigrant cultural identity and its role in familial expectations and dynamics. Also, this work shows the mental health effects of immigration on families, who usually experience trauma, abuse of all forms, and poverty.

Enrique's Journey by Sonia Nazario addresses the struggles of the unaccompanied children and youth attempting to cross the border, demonstrating the need to understand what drives thousands to make the journey.[10] This work portrays the indelible story of a

Honduran young man searching for his mother more than a decade after she was forced to abandon her starving family to find a better life in the United States. This incredible story allows us to dive into the mental ravages suffered by those who are victims of this dangerous odyssey.

GOD'S HOSPITALITY

What are God's thoughts regarding immigration? What is the Christian responsibility in the face of this phenomenon? Before answering these questions, it is important to give an overview of the main positions on this subject. On the one hand, we have the *exclusionists* whose narrative is to criminalize migrants to the point that they argue that immigrants are taking advantage of the goodness of the United States. On the other hand, there are the *inclusionists* whose narrative points out the vulnerability of the displaced and highlights their contributions. In the philosophical spectrum, we have *cosmopolitan* and *community* treatments of immigration. *Cosmopolitans* argue that the universal claims of human rights override the rights of nation-states to exclude migrants. *Communitarians* argue that the right of a political community to choose its own members is at the center of what it means to be a self-determining community. Philosophical ethics pursues questions such as, Under what circumstances can the migrant be admitted to a political community? or, When can citizenship be granted? Theological treatments of immigration, however, point out the perspective of the immigrant, their hopes, joys, suffering, resilience, and their families. This perspective argues that the immigrant experience has been ignored as a locus of theological reflection and that these experiences reveal genuine Christian theology. This perspective attempts to understand Christian theology using a hermeneutic interpretation of immigration. This perspective includes the contributions of liberation theology, born in Latin America. Usually, this perspective argues that political, social, and economic structures are unjust and sinful.[11]

Christian migration ethics has generally answered the question of responsibilities to non-citizens by affirming the full humanity of the displaced. All migrants are humans made in the image of God. Regardless of legal status or ethnicity, every individual bears the image of God.[12] We believe in a sovereign, transcendent, and immanent God, who created the heavens and the earth; God is actively working everything out for the good of God's people and God's glory. When we go to the Bible, we can constantly see how God's story uses immigration as a tool to accomplish his purposes on earth. God has used, and continues to use, the movement of people to radically change scenarios for nations and individuals. As Daniel G. Groody recalls, "Throughout the Judeo-Christian Scriptures migration is an inextricable link to God's covenant and our response."[13]

GOD'S MOVEMENT

God's activity is captured in the biblical narratives. Before the beginning of time, God has been the cause of the existence of all creation. Once God has spoken, the entire creation evolves according to God's purpose. This movement and activity of God described in the pages of the Bible is not limited to the moment of creation but continues until God completes his purposes for all creation. Salvation and redemption for all humanity is still a present purpose until Jesus Christ returns for a second time. Migration becomes a movement used by God to reach all nations. In the migratory phenomenon we can perceive the movement of God; in each immigrant there is a purpose dictated by God.

J. D. Payne defines migration as "the movement of people from location of residence to another location of residence and immigration is the movement of people into a different country to settle."[14] Through this movement of people, we can promptly see the activeness of God manifested in the phenomenon of migration. For Groody, a migrant is "any person who lives temporarily or permanently in a country where he or she was not born, and has acquired some significant social ties to this country."[15] Kent Annan defines an immigrant as "someone who has moved to another country for reasons that could include fleeing violence, natural disaster, or extreme poverty".[16] Also, Groody defines undocumented or irregular migrants as "people who enter a country usually in search of employment, without the necessary documents or permits."[17] A refugee "is someone who has been forced to flee his or her country because of persecution, war or violence,"[18] or "a person who, owing to well-founded fear of being persecuted for reasons of race, religion, nationality, membership of a particular social group or political opinion."[19] These definitions vary slightly, but all aim to identify an immigrant with someone moving from one place to another.[20]

All creation remains in constant motion, orchestrating God's command. Humanity is no exception, whether in the Mediterranean, in the Darien Gap, at the border between Mexico and the United States, or on any other migratory route. It does not matter if it is legal or illegal, voluntary or unvoluntary, that movement has a purpose for God's Salvation. All around the globe, God is reviving Christianity through the displaced.

Thomas Aquinas identifies God as the cause of all movement. Therefore, there would be no movement if it were not caused by God, the main agent to initiate that movement. In this way, the existence of movement, and the conclusion that everything that moves is moved by another, would demand the presence of a first force who, in this case, is God. In addition to that, the movement that arises from migration reminds us of the nature of God's kingdom: a kingdom that is constantly expanding throughout the earth. A movement that invites us to prepare to receive the guests that God is moving from other places to the United States to fulfil his purposes.

INVITATION INTO GOD'S STORY

From Genesis to Revelation, we can see the legitimation of God's care for immigrants. This legitimation should be our foundation as a church to always be proactive in our pastoral work toward documented or undocumented immigrants. Each person is a resemblance of God; therefore, we can contemplate God's image, the Triune God in dynamic unity and diversity.[21] There is a divine value in everyone: "so God created mankind in his own image, in the image of God he created them; male and female he created them" (Gen 1:27). Starting a theological reflection on immigration without having this biblical statement as foundation will lead us to take attitudes that denigrate the value and dignity of God's expression in every human being. "The act of dehumanizing lead us to awful places,"[22] but the perception of an immigrant as a real and clear image of God will take us beyond race, nation, or creed. "The creation of all persons in the image of God must be the most basic conviction for Christians as they approach the challenges of immigration today."[23]

Migration is the result of God's command: "Be fruitful and increase in number; fill the earth . . ." (Gen 1:28). In the pursuit of filling the earth, migration must take place in God's story. The movement of people from one place to another was not an afterthought in the mind of God. The migration of individuals to fill the earth of God's glory through proliferation and movement started from the beginning of creation.[24] The Genographic Project is perhaps one of the most recent studies providing a broader way to rediscover migration.[25] This project contours migration through the ages and provides a more concise idea of how migration has shaped our world as we know it: "such scientific discovery has given us an entirely new way of rediscovering that migration is literally in our genes."[26]

Genesis 1 gives prominence to the creation of the human race. The creation of man and woman is the climax of God's work. Male and female are made in the image of God. For Carroll, the image of God needs to be understood in a functional sense. Humans are designed to represent God on earth. This is not a passive representation; men and women are to direct over all things as God's vice-regents and take care of God's creation. Everyone is made in God's image and therefore has a singular standing before God and in the world.[27] Understanding this image of God as functional in humanity puts everyone on equal conditions, gives the same value to all, and elevates everyone to possess the same dignity for the simple fact that we are all God's creation. It makes us all stewards, representatives of God.

In Genesis 3:23 we have the first involuntary migration: "So the Lord God banished him [Cain] from the Garden of Eden." It is the result of a misguided decision. It is a movement from a permanent residence to a foreign land and begins the "chronicles of how migration [was] used to move the plan of salvation forward."[28] Cain responds to God expelling him from the land in Genesis 4:14: "Today you are driving me from the land, and I will be hidden from your presence; I will be a restless wanderer on the earth." With the fall, humanity begins moving away from God's image and likeness, from their true home, and from their integral connection to others. They become disconnected from God and from others. Human beings lose a sense of who they really are before God and who really are in relationship to others.[29]

Genesis 7:1 describes how perhaps the first refugees are told to "go into the ark, you and your whole family . . ." Noah's family is fleeing from violence and corruption. It was a family that was harassed for their religious beliefs: "by faith Noah" feared God's warning (Heb 11:7). It was his faith that led him to a new land. The wickedness around him was so great that it had reached heaven. God gave him the solution to flee from that violent land. The familiarity of their land, culture, and customs would be taken away and they would inhabit a new land. Then, in Genesis 10:30 we find "these are the clans of Noah's sons, according to their lines of descent, within their nations. From these the nations spread out over the earth after the flood." After the flood there was a great movement to multiply and fill the earth. "The descendants of Noah multiplied and spread across the earth."[30]

According to the text, Abraham heard God's voice: "The Lord had said to Abram, 'Go from your country, your people and your father's household to the land I will show you'" (Gen 12:1). Abram had a clear understanding of the reason why he was moving from one place to another. There was certainty in his heart about the journey he was about to begin, even though he did not have a clear path. This journey would demand trust amid hesitation, assurance amid disbelief, and surety amid insecure decisions. Abram's experience highlights how immigration contains complex levels of physical, psychological, social, and emotional vulnerability.[31] His migration was grounded on his faith, but that did not keep him from facing challenging ethical dilemmas along the way (Gen 12:11–20), nor scarcity of food or limitations due to the conditions of the land where he and his family were living at that time (Gen 12:10).

In Joseph's narrative, things are tremendously different as he was betrayed and sold as a slave by his own family (Gen 37). God used those events for him to become a nation: "but God sent me ahead of you to preserve for you a remnant on earth . . ." (Gen 45: 7). At first, and because of the tumultuous events in Joseph's life, no one would believe that God would use those unfortunate, traumatic, and suspicious events as a path to establish him as the second in command in Egypt. "So then, it was not you who sent me here, but God. He made me father to Pharaoh, lord of his entire household and ruler of all Egypt" (Gen 45:80). Joseph's narrative is important because it is perhaps the place where we find the first immigrant who, because of his faith in God, was able to assimilate a new culture and language from his new place of residence. Also, it was that same faith in God that allowed him to reinterpret the narrative of his life. The envy, rejections, betrayals, traumas, and conflicts were healed because Joseph was able to interpret his narrative from God's perspective. It is the life of Joseph that shows us the longings of those who are part of two countries, from two cultures and two languages. "Joseph is an illustration of the conflicted nature of many immigrants throughout the ages, who struggle with a heart for two cultures—the home culture and that of the host culture."[32]

The stories of Noah, Abraham, and Joseph each show us some aspects of how migration impacts families. The implications of embarking on a migratory journey can create great havoc in family life. In Noah's case, the harsh environment in which he lived implied seeking the preservation of himself and his family. In Abraham's case, it meant getting away from his nephew Lot for some time and lying about his relationship with Sarah. In the case of Joseph, it implied living apart from his family for a long time. As Carroll recalls, "the right to migrate is connected to the church's call to care for the vulnerable on the one hand, and to the human entitlement to dignity and the responsibility of providing for family on the other."[33] God instituted the family (Gen 2:18). In the Bible, we look at the family nucleus as something fundamental for God to carry out his purposes. The fulfillment of God's promises in Noah, Abraham, and Joseph always involves the family. Noah's family populated the earth after the flood, Abraham's family continued the development of God's promise to the patriarch, and Joseph's family gave rise to the birth of the nation of Israel.

In Genesis 2:18, we read "it is not good for man to be alone . . . ," which clearly shows the heart of a God interested in establishing a procreative society where individuals can experience his love, but also an integral structure to fulfill his purposes. Family is the central instrument in which God gives continuity to his purposes. "I will establish my covenant as an everlasting covenant between me and you and your descendants after you for the generations to come . . ." (Gen 17:7). When it comes to immigration, "laws that continue to needlessly separate families are problematic from a Christian perspective."[34] There are many critics of an immigration system that leads to "chain migration," where a person who becomes a citizen of the United States can sponsor an unlimited number of family members. The reality is that for many groups of immigrants, the process of sponsoring family members takes a long time. In my case, that process will take three to five additional years, after updating my immigration status in the United States. It was a twenty-three year wait to resolve my own immigration status and will be another three to five more years to be able to sponsor my parents. This adds up to about twenty-six to twenty-nine years. It is important for the church to begin to reflect on how we can minister to the families that are being affected by this very complex phenomenon of immigration. How can we fill the gaps left by family separation due to immigration? How do we help heal the dysfunctions created by this phenomenon? We do this while understanding the reality that the immigration system is far from perfect, and that legal or illegal migration will not stop.

Turning to the plight of communities, in Exodus, we find the closest phenomenon to what today would be the caravans of migrants who come mainly from Latin America. After being liberated from Egypt, Israel's journey to another land began. God used Moses to guide Israel through the desert; then, after more than forty years and more than five thousand miles away from Egypt, Joshua conquered the promised land. The caravan of Israelites flees from oppression by the Egyptian government. "They made their lives bitter with harsh labor in brick and mortar and with all kinds of work in the fields; in all their harsh labor the Egyptians worked them ruthlessly" (Exod 1:14). Interestingly, later in the narrative it tells us that God listened to the pain of God's people. "God heard their groaning, and he remembered his covenant with Abraham, with Isaac and with Jacob. So, God looked on the Israelites and was concerned about them" (Exod 2:24–25). All this movement arises from many people longing for better living conditions. God is concerned about them and heard their groaning, and then, God prepared the logistics, the leader, and displayed the power to lead the people to conquer a land where there was abundance.

In the exodus, we notice many parallels with today's conditions. Although the context of the biblical narrative is very different from ours, there are two elements that do not change: God, and a multitude of individuals crying out for a better life. "In the end, the exodus is a human story about the search for dignity, freedom, and life."[35] The liberation of Israel becomes a fundamental model to understand all aspects of the phenomenon of migration. Not only is it a geographic movement, but it has social, psychological, and spiritual implications. Furthermore, the exodus shows us a God who cares about the oppressed and a God who cares about immigrants: "do not mistreat or oppress a foreigner, for you were foreigners in Egypt" (Exod 22:21).

Around 722 BC, God's people were forced to live far from their land and their people by the Assyrians. "So the people of Israel were taken from their homeland into exile in Assyria . . ." (2 Kgs 17:23). Then, around 597 BC, Nebuchadnezzar, "carried all Jerusalem into exile: all the officers and fighting men, and all the skilled workers and artisans . . ." (2 Kgs 24:14). These events in the life and existence of the nation of Israel show us the implications and effects of those who are displaced due to war. The periods of exile of the nation of Israel not only describe those who were forced to migrate but also shows us the life and assimilation of the new culture of the new generations of Israelites; and more than that, it shows us a God interested in the welfare of the displaced. "This is what the Lord Almighty, the God of Israel, says to all those I carried into exile from Jerusalem to Babylon: Build houses and settle down; plant gardens and eat what they produce. Marry and have sons and daughters; find wives for your sons and give your daughters in marriage, so that they too may have sons and daughters. Increase in number there; do not decrease. Also, seek the peace and prosperity of the city to which I have carried you into exile. Pray to the Lord for it, because if it prospers, you too will prosper" (Jer 29:4–7). Jeremiah counsels the exiles to invest in their new land. This was a call to accommodate to their new context. Despite their limitations and powerlessness, they could continue be instruments of God.[36]

The new generations of Jews born in exile give us an idea of what would be the second generation of immigrants in the United States today: individuals who are part of two worlds, but who do not belong to either. They cannot be considered part of the dominant culture because their ancestors are part of minorities, nor can they be considered 100 percent citizens of their parents' country of origin. "Their identity as Jews would be experienced in a different way."[37]

In the Old Testament we find plenty of material that portrays the fate and feelings of those experiencing the effects of being far away from their homeland. They are the longings of those who, by God's design, have had to experience that difficult journey away from their land, and live with the expectation, and the hope, of one day seeing their land blessed, restored and prosperous. Nehemiah suffered the longing of the ones left behind: "those who survived the exile and are back in the province are in great trouble and disgrace. The wall of Jerusalem is broken down, and its gates have been burned with fire. When I heard these things, I sat down and wept. For some days I mourned and fasted and prayed . . ." (Neh 1:3–4). The psalmist writes, "When the Lord restored the fortunes of Zion, we were like those who dreamed. Our mouths were filled with laughter, our tongues with songs of joy" (Ps 126:1–2). There was a deep desire to go back to their land: "When the Lord restores his people, let Jacob rejoice and Israel be glad!" (Ps 14:7, 53:6). "'The days are coming,' declares the Lord, 'when I will bring my people Israel and Judah back from captivity and restore them'" (Jer 30:3). "Also, for you, Judah, a harvest is appointed. Whenever I would restore the fortunes of my people . . ." (Hos 6:11).

Prophetic activity was also carried out through immigrants. "Many of the great Old Testament prophets lived as immigrants and foreign captives, Jeremiah, Ezekiel, Daniel, Ezra, Nehemiah, and others."[38] Unfortunately, the period in which these prophets lived was a time of judgment for the nation of Israel. The nation did not repent of their evil ways and sins, and as a nation, they were living the consequences of moving away from God. If we are consistent with our theological approach, many of God's accusations toward the nation had to do with their relationship with God, and their treatment of their neighbor in the sociopolitical life of the nation. My hope is that as a church, we can understand what God is saying through the many immigrant prophets that God has brought to the United States.

God's purpose for Israel was to be a light to the nations of the earth. Because of that, God commanded them to live, behave, and think differently than the rest of the world. In that formation of a nation according to God's heart, the immigrant had to be cared for in a specific way. However, Israel failed to maintain that distinction between those who know of God and those who do not. "If you really change your ways and your actions and deal with each other justly, if you do not oppress the foreigner . . . then I will let you live in this place" (Jer 7:5–7).

WELCOMING INTO GOD'S KINGDOM

In the New Testament, God proposes a new model of government, a model that is not restricted to borders established by humans. This is a model that transcends territories, a government that is carried in the heart, a model that continues to promote dignified treatment for immigrants. It is also a model that invites us to think of ourselves as pilgrims, as people who are passing through. Although we are in the world, we are not of this world (Heb 13:14). The New Testament constantly reminds us of what our eternity will be like in heavenly dwellings. It is a kingdom that proposes Jesus Christ as King. Jesus calls it the kingdom of heaven. In that timeless and indestructible kingdom all earthly things, ethnic traits, and ideals are surrendered at the feet of the King of kings. The divine constitution of that kingdom makes us all brothers and sisters, sons and daughters. It gives the same value and dignity to all of us. It makes us part of a body, where we are all indispensable.

The New Testament presents some images for the believers intended to prevent the fragmentation of the church, a fragmentation that could occur due to the incorporation of new ethnic groups into the church or displacement due to persecution. The first image is that of the body of Christ. The second is the family of God, and the third is the divine citizenship. We find the emerging church being dispersed, forced to take refuge in places outside Jerusalem because they were persecuted for their religious beliefs. "On that day a great persecution broke out against the church in Jerusalem" (Acts 8:1). Since its founding, the church has survived by its identity as a divine entity that has the capacity to integrate all people of different languages and nations. "For we were all baptized by one Spirit so as to form one body, whether Jews or Gentiles, slave or free . . ." (1 Cor 12:13). We find a divine entity with an identity not defined by any external element, but by the Holy Spirit that is poured out on us. Our identity is formed by the Holy Spirit. In the formation of that identity, the Holy Spirit with his divine essence will reform our psychological conception, will disrupt our cultural values to teach us how to build a new divine culture. He will reshape our social relationships with his divine hospitality and will change our hearts to make us a different nation.

The Pauline letters refer to the church as the body of Christ. "Transcending all borders, this body binds all people together through love. This love also calls them to remember especially those who have been displaced from the body of society, like the poor, the vulnerable, and the forgotten."[39] This image of the church as the body of Christ provides the church with an identity that nullifies all social and ethnic differences. It presents us with a reality of equality, dignity, and functionality expressed in diversity and love.

In the New Testament we can see the same trinity from the Old Testament providing a savior and place to remind us that we are all created in the image of God. Paul continues to use the image of the family that we find in Genesis as an instrument to fulfill God's purposes for the church. Matthew Soerens and Jenny Yang, in *Welcoming the Stranger* put it this way: "Now we have been naturalized into God's kingdom and adopted into his family through the blood of Jesus Christ."[40] And Ephesians 2:19 says, "Consequently, you are no longer foreigners and strangers, but fellow citizens with God's people and also members of his household."

In its countercultural nature, the image of divine citizenship becomes an anchor for the emerging church due to its constant struggle not to conform to the world; rather, "our citizenship is in heaven. And we eagerly await a Savior from there, the Lord Jesus Christ" (Phil 3:20). According to Daniel Groody, "It speaks to the belief that this world has never been, never is, and never can be a final destination or a lasting home, which means that migration is at the core of Christian identity."[41] In his monumental work *The City of God*, Augustine of Hippo refers to the nature of the kingdom of heaven. He does it at a time when the Roman empire is in decline. "While this Heavenly City, therefore, is on pilgrimage in this world she calls out citizens from all nations, and so collects a society of pilgrims, speaking all languages."[42]

The first epistle of Peter continues to shape the emerging church's worldview on immigration. Peter uses different terms that refer to what our citizenship in heaven implies. The recipients of the letter are called *foreigners* and *strangers*. Παρεπιδήμοις (*parepídēmos*)—a sojourner (foreigner)—is literally someone *passing through*, but still with a personal relationship with the people in that locale. This temporary (but active) relationship is made necessary by circumstances. Παροίκους (*pároikos*) is a stranger, properly, someone living close to others as a temporary dweller in a specific place as a non-citizen with limited rights.[43] According to M. Daniel Carroll R., "These outsiders were not granted the rights and privileges of a full citizenship, and so they had to endure economic, political, and social limitations."[44] By using these words Peter lays the foundation for those who adhere to the kingdom of heaven not to focus on earthly things that can create a division among them.

The Scriptures not only tell us to welcome and care for immigrants but also command us to obey and respect the law created by the governing authorities. That is the dilemma presented by Romans 13:1: "Let everyone be subject to the governing authorities, for there is no authority except that which God has established. The authorities that exist have been established by God." If our goal as part of the kingdom of heaven is to seek God's justice, then we should ask ourselves if the laws established by our authorities honor God's justice. When the laws prevent us from fulfilling God's justice, our response should be like that of Peter and John: "Which is right in God's eyes: to listen to you, or to him? You be the judges!" (Acts 4:19). Ultimately, the law must answer God's higher law, which requires us to treat all human life with sanctity. All persons bear God's image and thus should be treated with dignity.[45]

The scenarios in the biblical narrative where this movement of people takes place are incredibly different, but there is one common denominator in all of them: God using that movement to accomplish his purposes. Perhaps we need to start approaching migration not as a part of a bordered and fragmented world, but as part of God's kingdom, which transcends borders and bonds people for his purposes.

ALIENS AS GUESTS IN THE BIBLE

Currently, the term *illegal alien* refers to an individual who does not hold a legal status in the United States. This designation is the beginning of the debate because, for some, the connotation of *alien* might refer to an extraterrestrial character in a science fiction series. However, when we scrutinize the historical meaning of the concept, we notice that it has gradually evolved. About six hundred years ago the term was used to distinguish between the free and unfree. This concept has grown to refer to someone worthy of suspicion. The *alien* refers to someone outside of the faith and allegiance of the king. It carries an implication of suspicion, someone to be distrusted. For theologian Robert Heimburger this concept of *alien* makes US federal immigration law possible. The term *alien* had been increasingly isolated in legal language, carrying an overtone of suspicion. For US immigration law, the *alien* becomes someone whose entrance into the US territory may be restricted. In the first century of the American republic, the Supreme Court justified the right to exclude and expel aliens based on the sovereignty, self-preservation, and self-defense of the nation.[46]

Ethicist Dana Wilbanks suggests that the terms *undocumented worker* or *undocumented migrant* convey the recognition of the immigrant as a human being. For him, these terms communicate more accurately that these immigrants are in the country without legal documentation without denigrating or dangerously suggesting these individuals are not human beings.[47] Considering that most immigrants embrace the Christian faith, Joseph Castleberry proposes to call them the *new pilgrims*. Pilgrim refers to a traveler or wanderer, especially in a foreign place or a newcomer to a region or place.[48]

The Bible uses different words to refer to a migrant or immigrant. Most scholars agree that the Hebrew word *gêr* refers to someone who moves from another place to take up residence. The *gêr*, the stranger, is thus one who can be joined to Israel, more like an immigrant than a foreigner.[49] For the scholars, based on textual, historical, and archeological evidence, *gêr* refers to a person not native to the local area and without family or land.[50] An Israelite citizen is referred to as a countryman *ach* in Scripture, whereas a legal immigrant is referred to as a sojourner, a *gêr*.[51]

As part of the kingdom of God we need to resist the temptation to undervalue people. Karl Barth thinks that a person is freed by the divine command to come near to those nearby and those far away. For him, migrants are not fundamentally different from those who are more settled among people; all travel in the pilgrim's way. They may be near, or they may be far, but they are near neighbors or distant neighbors.[52] In the story of God, the displaced is not a secondary actor, but rather becomes the protagonist.

BELONGING AND OPEN ARMS FOR THE DISPLACED

Theologians have already laid a robust foundation on which we can begin to equip our congregations. There is a saying in Mexico: *tenemos mucha tela de donde cortar*.[53] In his broad manner of administering God's grace, Jesus always displayed a high standard of justice and mercy toward those who had been displaced from their circle within society or their place in a community. In the biblical narrative, meeting Jesus is to return to a place of belonging, to a place where dignity is recovered, a place where the divine value of the individual is recovered and is not limited to earthly possessions or social circles. The displaced belong to God's family and are adopted as children of God. The subjects in this case are individuals who are actively seeking the full recognition of the dignity of their humanity.[54] Paul had that in mind when he wrote to the Galatians, "There is no longer Jew or Greek; there is no longer slave or free; there is no longer male and female, for all of you are one in Christ Jesus" (Gal 3:28).

Jesus transforms all the earthly and fragmented paradigms, fragmented because of the invisible borders we have created with each other. Jesus points toward the heavenly horizon, where there are no borders, no divisions, no exclusions. A place where everyone is welcome, where everyone belongs to everyone, where the more distant becomes my closest neighbor. It is a movement that actively seeks out the vulnerable person who reminds us we are constantly in the process of becoming and making ourselves a neighbor.[55]

For a fifteen-year-old young man who had no one, who had suffered terribly on his migratory journey to this country and who was forming an identity, the fact of coming to church and being adopted, cared for, and accepted, healed my heart. It gave me a new perspective, changed my narrative, and reminded me of the place I have in God's heart. We often forget how powerful is the community life that the church promotes. We are not just any organization; there is divine, healing power that flows from us as God's people.

THE SPIRIT WITH NO BORDERS

Before Christ ascended into heaven, he ordered his disciples not to go out of Jerusalem. "He gave them this command: Do not leave Jerusalem, but wait for the gift my Father promised" (Acts 1:4). Before they could go out, it was necessary for the Holy Spirit to come in. "But you will receive power when the Holy Spirit comes on you; and you will be my witnesses in Jerusalem, and in all Judea and Samaria, and to the ends of the earth" (Acts 1:8). Following the biblical narrative, the event of the outpouring of the Spirit is what we know as Pentecost. "All of them were filled with the Holy Spirit and began to speak in other tongues as the Spirit enabled them" (Acts 2:4). At that moment the era of the Spirit was inaugurated, an era where the territorial borders would have no authority to determine the development of the church. No human restriction, nor persecution will be able to stop what the Spirit was doing.

It is important to reflect that the mobilizing power of the church does not depend on human virtue itself. Rather, it emerges from the divine essence that transcends all earthly forces that consciously or unconsciously try to stop the progress of the kingdom of heaven. Pentecost becomes a calling for all nations, a calling to become part of the kingdom of heaven. Therefore, no human barrier, be it a border, language, culture, or ethnicity, can stop it, nor is anyone exempt from that call. The Spirit penetrates impenetrable borders, disrupting systems that corrupt the unity and dignity of God's creation. The Holy Spirit is not racist, nor discriminatory. It is a Spirit that has no favorites. It is a Spirit that works for an eternity where people of all towns and nations dwell together.

For Heimburger, the Spirit who sends out the church and ensures its apostolicity makes possible a new solidarity with migrants. This solidarity means that the simple and unqualified term *alien* is not a true term for a believer. These encounters with fellow migrants play a part in saving the church by reminding us of its missionary character.[56] These encounters with the migrant church give the geopolitical context a new horizon. It breaks all homogeneity as a result of an earthly nationalism, and gives rise to human diversity within the church, but dependent and united by the Holy Spirit. This dependency of the Spirit gives rise to a new spiritual revolution that leads us to new missionary journeys in future generations.

GOD SPEAKS OUR LANGUAGE

I arrived in the United States at the age of fifteen. Unfortunately, I was not able to attend school and learn the language properly. As of today, I continue to learn it and still do not feel completely capable of communicating in English. The helplessness of not being able to communicate properly is one of the most frustrating sensations I have ever felt. The inability to communicate can prevent us from establishing solid and trusting relationships.

Language is an important element in the dynamics of belonging, in part because it is such a central mediator of culture.[57] Belonging is the result of being loved, and it plays a fundamental role in our emotional and psychological well-being. As we grow up, we seek acceptance and affection from those around us, whether in our family relationships, friendships, or romantic partners. These needs drive us to form strong and meaningful bonds with others and provide us with a sense of identity and belonging in the world. The Christian principle is that love is God, or more exactly, that God is love, agape, or charity.

The American church speaks English and Hispanics speak Spanish. But I would like to suggest that while we learn the two beautiful languages, we also start communicating in a more sublime language. The language that surpasses any earthly language. The language that will remain after eternity. The language that emulates God, the language of love. God is love, and if we begin to speak love, then, we will communicate in God's language. Love put into practice transcends languages. Our intentions and actions are understood without the need to communicate it through words. An action speaks louder than a thousand words and actions transcend languages. Speaking love is to identify ourselves with the vulnerable, with the weak, not because we are strong or not vulnerable, but because we recognize these elements in ourselves. Identification with what they live in the periphery implies putting aside the power, status, or the privileges that separate us.[58]

If we really want to embrace the reality of a catholic or universal church, love will be the language we use to show God's heart. It is the intensity of love we put into our gestures, attitudes and actions that will tell our neighbors how much God loves them. God wants us to love one another and give ourselves to each other. It does not matter how many words we speak, but how much love we put in our actions. For us to love, we need to have faith because faith is love in action; and love in action is service. The fruit of love is service. Love constantly leads us to offer ourselves in sacrifice. Our sacrifice brings reconciliation, peace, and unity.[59]

Christians should discard any language as a limit for their communication of the good news. Love transcends any social structure and creates community. The racial and ethnic diversity of the United States means that Christians are not allowed to ignore or forget other ways of being the Church. A multicultural and multiracial Church needs a much greater language to avoid national identity to influence who can be considered part of the church or not. Our God speaks all languages, but it is God's love that unites people from races and nations.⁶⁰

Love means expanding our hearts and joyfully accepting the calvary that lies ahead of us, conscious of the salvation that comes after that sacrifice. Love is expressed through fervor. The loss of it may lead the church into enthusiasm about other tasks that fail to demonstrate the love of God.⁶¹ The immigration reality invites us to focus on God's desire for his church in this nation. Focusing on God's will involves denying ourselves to take up a cross. Taking up the cross implies a certain discomfort that can lead us to lose the fervor with which we serve our neighbor. The way to expand our hearts to love others joyfully is by living and speaking love. Love never fails.

UNDOCUMENTED THEOLOGY

Years of living as an undocumented person and having the privilege of experiencing an academic formation at Azusa Pacific University and Fuller Theological Seminary have allowed me to reflect on the God who does not leave you and does not turn his back even if you are considered a fugitive. In the darkest moments of a pilgrimage as an undocumented migrant, God did not look at me or treat me differently. In fact, he was the one who walked closest with me because I was the one who needed him the most. The narrative of the thief on the cross amazes me because it displays the mystery of the multiform grace of God (Luke 23:39–42). On the one hand, we have someone who, according to the legal system of that time, deserved to be labeled, denigrated, and treated as a thief. On the other hand, we have one who had not committed any crime, but that same legal system had convicted him, and therefore he would carry the same labels as another thief. It is in that contradiction of the legal system of that time where we can observe the mysterious, compassionate God's approach and company for those who have lost their dignity.

There, in those marginalized places where the voiceless live, a place where no one expected something great to happen, the God who does not judge the same as humans appears. Jesus could have ignored the dialogue that these two criminals had. After all, one of them was attacking his dignity. The other rebuked his partner and recognized that they were there because they had done wrong things, but that Jesus did not have to be there. Jesus does not ignore the voice of the voiceless but listens. At the end of the day, whether Jesus deserved to be there or not didn't matter, because under the legal system of that time, the three of them had to be there and die. And that is where the scandalous and irrational aspect of the gospel appears. In this event, only an exchange of glances and a request were enough for this marginalized criminal to discover the scandalous grace of the kingdom of God. Almost on his last breath, the thief imagines a place where even people who have been labeled like him can belong. A place that transcends what is known and established. A place of inclusion for the repentant. Jesus does promise him that his words have been heard and that he will enjoy that place of belonging.

God does not need our legitimacy to fulfill his purposes. No matter how scandalous it is, time and time again, the Bible displays a God who crosses, invades, or even exterminates nations to fulfill his purposes. Among many other narratives, the exodus narrative shows this concept of God empowering the voiceless, the marginalized, or the strangers to create something new. The creation of the new implies breaking with what is established by the authorities and which is therefore considered legitimate. For the structures or systems that ensure what is legitimate, God can be dangerous, especially if these human-structured systems have forgotten the inclusion of the most vulnerable.

The vulnerable may be the displaced, those who are homeless, those who do not meet the requirements established by what is legally legitimate. God overlooks legitimate structures so that from what is considered undocumented and illegitimate he continues to imagine new spaces where everyone has a place.

In those suspicious, ignored places of suffering and complexity is where undocumented theology arises. At least, that's what happened to Moses; as a fugitive, he fled to the desert, where God called him, and after that, the exiled became a liberator. Or there is Saul of Tarsus (Paul), who legally violated the rights of religious expression of his time, persecuting the emerging church until God called him. After that, the persecutor became the persecuted. The examples of Moses, Jesus, and Paul are precise ways to express what God does from what can be considered suspicious or outside the law. In all the examples, God created something new: a new nation with Moses, a new kingdom with Jesus, and the expansion of his church with Paul.

These suspicious spaces forgotten by the cat's whiskers of society become places where, due to the very precarious conditions, the undocumented—with Bible in hand, because it is the only thing that is not denied to them—begin to imagine, together with God, those utopias of the kingdom. Their faith becomes hope and imagination. Because they experience so many shortcomings, God becomes everything: their home, their country, their food, and their judge. The undocumented learn to look at the expressions of God in the margins, a God who breaks social, economic, and cultural categories to shape a new society not based on possessions, abilities, or races, but simply on the fact that all have been created by him.

This is the reflection of those who have been classified as illegitimate and seek their identity in the one who is the creator of everything. Of the exiles who raise their gaze toward a land that transcends the earthly. The dispossessed who cling to an incorruptible and unfading treasure. The resistance of those who hunger and thirst for justice. It is the longing of a new place where all the injustices created by a broken humanity are destroyed. In this theocracy, everyone has a place, everyone is a child of God, everyone is a creation of God, and everyone has the same worth.

For the undocumented theologian the foundation is the kingdom of heaven presented by Jesus Christ. It is a non-violent kingdom by nature, a kingdom that historically, constantly challenges established systems. It is a kingdom that cannot be subjected to, or linked to a human regime; it is by nature divine, and that is where its complexity lies. It has been clearly described in the teachings of Jesus Christ but has not been put into practice by any human government—not even by those who call themselves a Christian nation. Perhaps we have seen glimpses of the kingdom of heaven in some constitutions or policies of some nations, but they are just that, glimpses.

There are two entities or agents where, biblically, the kingdom of God should be more visible: the church and the so-called Christians. But despite all the biblical empowerment and guidance, even these two have not been able to fully reflect the majesty of the kingdom of God in their midst. The ideals of the kingdom are too high and complex for our still corrupted and power-hungry humanity. Although there are tangible images of the kingdom in some places, we still have a lot to develop to make the kingdom more visible than theoretical. For now, all that remains is to continue resisting everything that is not compatible with the kingdom of heaven. Someday, as Paul says, the creation will be liberated from its bondage to decay and brought into freedom and glory.

CHAPTER THREE

Psychological Needs in the Immigrant Community

There could be several reasons why a person or a whole family decides to leave their country, whether voluntarily or involuntarily. Those reasons can be personal or family related and may be to seek work opportunities or economic aspirations, or to avoid political oppression, war conflicts, religious persecution, natural disaster, or other calamities. If there is a country or destination that can help alleviate the reasons why you leave your homeland and offers you the opportunity for a better life, then those possibilities of a better life become a reason for why a country might attract immigrants. Everything lies in the fundamental reason of migrants seeking a better quality of life for themselves or their families.

Although the volume of literature regarding immigration has increased, and the economic, political, labor, and social implications of immigration have been studied broadly, very little has been discussed about the psychological and emotional implications affecting the migrant as an individual. I believe it is extremely important to address the consequences of the losses experienced by migrants and the psychological effects we suffer after that journey. The mental health of the displaced can be tremendously affected after exposure to extreme situations. As the hosting church, we cannot ignore the psychological reality the displaced face when arriving in the United States.

In chapter 1, I mentioned the common attitude of Hispanics about going to the doctor, *el matasanos*. Why should I go to the doctor if they don't do anything for me? On the contrary, I'll get worse. This same type of attitude is very common regarding psychological care: *ni que estuviera loco*. Conversations about psychological intervention in Hispanics are not common, especially within the first generation. When the word psychologist is mentioned in a conversation, many Hispanics assume that they are being called crazy, and that is why they reject the idea of consulting a psychologist. I have even heard Hispanic ministers in pulpits preach about the rejection of seeking psychological care, arguing that whoever has Christ and goes to a psychologist despises the sacrifice of Christ that has made us a new creature. This conception of medical care prevents us from looking at the reality of a people who suffer in silence.

WHAT WE DO NOT PERCEIVE AT FIRST SIGHT

We immigrants carry scars on our bodies that remind us of what it meant to come to this country. Some of us have suffered a physical injury or lost a limb. A few years ago, I had the opportunity to meet an undocumented young man who had lost his hand while traveling on the train *La Bestia* in Mexico. Most Central American immigrants use this means of transportation to reach the border of the United States and Mexico. But we also carry wounds that are not visible at first sight. They are the wounds of the soul, the sufferings that we keep in the deepest recesses of our hearts. They are wounds that are more difficult to heal. This is where the local church becomes a light on the hill, a source of life, a refuge for the weary.

Immigrants everywhere will experience loss, grief, and mourning. To one degree or another, these elements are part of the migration experience. In comparison to death, the grief of migration can be both more extensive and more limited. It can be extensive because family members and friends stay behind. Familiar language, customs, food, and comforting identification with their culture are gone. Such grief can also be limited because the losses are not clear, complete, or irretrievable. Immigration is a stressful life event, and refugees, displaced persons, and immigrants inevitably suffer significant emotional distress.[1] Migration indeed is a disruptive experience; it is important to recognize and be aware of the enormous amount of stress a displaced person might endure in the process of adaptation. Having the necessary information, acquiescing, and sensitizing ourselves will lead to better understanding of how to pastor and accompany the displaced in their process of incorporation into the new culture.

We, the displaced live in a limbo: on the one hand, we lose everything with which we identify, and on the other hand, we are placed in a new context where we can gain other things that will enrich our lives. However, we will always live in that dichotomy, between our native land and this new context. In this new context, the displaced might find a community or neighborhood that reproduces sounds, smells, or tastes of one's hometown. All these elements will create a significant mix of emotions: sadness for the losses, but joy for the gains. Affliction for the significant achievements made while away from those who stayed behind, but contentment for the achievements that have helped those who stayed behind. The migrant exists in a world of the incomplete, postponed, ambiguous and longing.[2]

The first phase in the migration journey is leaving one's homeland. Regardless of the classification given to the person—displaced, emigrant, asylum seeker, immigrant, etc.—the common feature in any station of this journey is trauma. Trauma might be defined here as psychic or spiritual injury experienced by fear. Trauma can be a temporary experience of shock or loss, but in some instances the experience becomes ongoing and severe to the point of disabling the person in terms of normal functioning in society. At that point, it may be an instance of what is medically called post-traumatic stress disorder (PTSD). In the case of PTSD, the person may experience recurrent, intrusive flashbacks of memory of the event that caused the stress and symptoms may include irritability, nervousness, inability to sleep or relax and, in some instances, PTSD can even lead to death.

In severe cases of PTSD, psychological and medical interventions are required. The second phase in the migration journey is the transition to the new situation, and this creates a second set of challenges for the displaced. In the case of those who migrate voluntarily through established legal channels, the bureaucracy and complexity of the process may leave scars. For those who migrate involuntarily, it involves a more complex process, and depending on the given situation, this will affect the assimilation and acculturation of the individual. In the third phase, the displaced must settle into their new situation. This settlement process can take a long time, and even then, the migrant will never fully settle in the new context.[3]

In most countries and throughout history, immigrants and asylum seekers have experienced formal or informal prejudice. Sometimes they also experience discrimination because they are not able to communicate properly or because of the lack of assimilation to the new culture. The displaced are stigmatized, stereotyped, and forced to walk in the margins of our societies.[4] From experience, it is demeaning being the only one asked to show an ID because you look suspicious. It is disparaging when police pull you over, arguing that you do not look familiar to the neighborhood profile.

For psychologist Celia Jaes Falicov, the displaced experience three uprootings: physical, social, and cultural. The physical uprooting comes with the disruption of the homeland. It entails living without the familiarity of everything the individual feels comfortable with. The social uprooting comes with disruptions and reconstitutions of the social network. It is very common that displaced people will incline toward neighborhoods that maximize contact with conationals. The cultural uprooting, or the classic term *culture shock*, comes when meanings are changed or lost. There is an abrupt exposure to a new language, new customs, new lifestyles, and new values that precipitates psychological distress.[5]

The initial conception of most people who immigrate to the United States is that it is a dream of equality, opportunity, and fairness. However, once they have arrived in the country, the sociopolitical reality differs from what was initially conceived. The immigrant realizes the division and tensions that exist between anti-immigration and pro-immigration groups. In addition to that, there is a lack of recognition and appreciation for the work they do and the economic contribution they generate. For example, during the Covid-19 pandemic, one group of essential workers that received little or no recognition was fieldworkers, most of whom are undocumented immigrants.

Another factor we must take into consideration is the perception or stereotype that we have of each person or race. In psychology, this perception of each other is known as social categories. They affect the way we see each other, but it's important to understand that social categories are constructed; they are not natural entities. Understanding these categories will help us to understand the way we interact with our world around us.[6] The displaced have none of the material evidence of the so-called American Dream, and they have had few if any experiences of achievement. The result might be feelings of inferiority and inadequacy that are deeply rooted and all pervasive.[7] More than anything, comprehending these constructed categories can be a great tool for understanding how members of marginalized groups deal with discrimination, suffering, stereotyping, trauma, and other stressors. The sociohistorical experience of the displaced has contributed to the development of a sense of unworthiness, and sociocultural alterations and losses may seriously harm identity in the individual.[8]

Recently, all of us have witnessed the humongous multitude of *carabanas* from Central America. Immigration is becoming increasingly relevant for a world that is becoming more diverse.[9] Within this diversity of migrants we find professionals, or people who in their countries had a good lifestyle but due to circumstances beyond their control had to leave their homeland. In addition to that, there are many immigrants who profess our faith. As a hosting church we need to be cautious and not categorize migrant in the same way the world does. Our perception of the undocumented immigrant should not be based on a social category, especially if they profess our faith. This is a real challenge since biblically, in the church there is only the category of Christ. In order to create welcome and inclusion for the displaced it is important to heal, restore, and dignify those whom society has marginalized and oppressed.[10]

In contrast to social categories, social identity refers to those traits and behaviors that the person finds self-descriptive. Social identification plays a significant role in one's happiness, satisfying needs for self-esteem, self-coherence, and belonging. Social identification has important implications for affect, cognition, and behavior.[11] The displaced person is searching for an identity that has been affected by his or her migration experience. Many of us feel that our past is cut off, our present is confusing, and we do not know what our future will be.[12]

This identity relates to how we identify ourselves in relation to others according to what we have in common. It can provide us with a sense of self-esteem and a framework for socializing, and it can influence our behavior. When we perceive identity threats, we can experience involuntary stress responses. These responses are emotional, cognitive, physiological, and behavioral, including increased anxiety, elevated blood pressure, and reduced working memory capacity.[13] In the case of Hispanics, their identity is in formation. Mixed, confused, or undefined, every day more elements come to light that shape that identity, based on context and nationality.[14] One must consider the person in the situation and context. Context is the surrounding environment for situations. The importance of context is essential to understand the complexity and variability of social behavior.[15]

Another reality for Hispanics is their efforts to overcome a feeling of marginality. It is a double marginalization, on the one hand, by the dominant culture of the new nation, and on the other, by their own nation. Therefore, Hispanics are struggling to overcome the various dimensions of this state of relegation that afflict their lives.[16] We never will understand the needs of the stigmatized, displaced, or undocumented immigrants from the perspective of unstigmatized or advantaged members of society. Approaching from this perspective will lead us to a pervasiveness of prejudice and discrimination against people on the margins of society. Members of stigmatized groups experience a variety of forms of interpersonal rejection, such as being slighted, ignored, excluded, patronized, belittled, ridiculed, and targeted by violence. Because psychological well-being is at least partly dependent on inclusion by others and perception that one is valued by others, interpersonal threats can have profoundly negative psychological implications for their targets.[17] When the displaced arrive in the new context, they do not belong to anyone, and yet belonging is a prerequisite for mental health. There is a sense of isolation and aloneness that characterizes the displaced.[18]

Taking all these psychological aspects into account will help us to be a welcoming church aware of the possible needs of all those who have been displaced. What follows is a list of the most common psychological effects experienced by migrants. Also, we need to remember that each migration story is different, with different traumatic events and different suffering situations.

THE ULYSSES SYNDROME

In 2002, Dr. Joseba Achotegui was the first to use the term *Ulysses Syndrome* to describe all the mourning symptoms experienced by migrants. According to Achotegui, there are seven forms of migratory mourning that affect the mental health of immigrants in relevant and tangible ways. Greek mythology describes Ulysses as a character who survived terrible adversities and dangers. The current migrations parallel the odysseys the poet describes of someone pushing forward despite the challenges to survive. The Ulysses syndrome functions as a thermometer within the mental health context gauging between mental health problems and mental health diseases. Metaphorically speaking, this syndrome can be understood as being in a room where the temperature rises to 100 degrees centigrade. Our body would begin to experience vertigo, headaches, or other symptoms, not because we are sick but as the body's response to extreme conditions.[19]

The seven forms of migratory mourning affecting the mental health of migrants are:

1. *Family and loved ones*: the uncertainty of not knowing when they will be reunited.
2. *Language*: if language is different, it will be more difficult to adapt.
3. *Culture*: conflicts between the migrant's own culture and the new culture make adaptation more difficult.
4. *Homeland*: unfamiliar places or temperatures can cause stress.
5. *Social Status*: adaptation to lower socioeconomic conditions may increase stress levels.
6. *Group belonging*: the migrant may feel uncomfortable when seeing or interacting with different ethnicities.
7. *Physical risk*: the migrant may experience dangers, suffering, or abuses.

CONTINUED STRESS

I pastor a couple who lived for at least two years in a single room. It was literally a room with a small kitchen and a bathroom. The owner had arranged this room for one person to live in. When this couple arrived in the country it was the only place they found, and due to the urgency, they had to move in. The husband worked night shifts, and the wife sometimes worked in the morning. On top of that, they had a seven-year-old son. Recently, I had the opportunity to bring some furniture to the new place they moved into. They now live in a one-bedroom apartment. When I asked them about how they feel in their new apartment, they shared how frustrating and complicated it was to live in that small room as a family. They shared with me that many times the wife had to wear a headlamp to be able to cook or clean the room because her husband had to sleep and needed to have the lights off. Later in the conversation they mentioned that now they worried about paying rent, as they are paying more for the new place, and the wife has not been able to find a job that fits her schedule since she has to drop off and pick up her son from school.

A few months ago, a young couple who had recently arrived in the country rented a room where they share a bathroom, kitchen, and living room with another family. In one of our meetings for their baptism classes, the wife shared with me that they were very frustrated because coexistence in that house is very complicated. The person in charge of the house demands a lot from them and insinuates things about her husband. Since the husband was released from the detention center, the husband has been wearing a shackle, and for fear of being deported they had decided not to start looking for a job for the moment.

These two stories reflect the day-to-day lives of many immigrants. The settlement process is a very complicated process. The lack of resources and space creates stress for the displaced. If unemployment and lack of funds continue, levels of stress might increase. Continued stress creates tension, and if tension is not properly managed the result will be bitterness. Bitterness inevitably will affect personality.[20]

THE LEFT BEHIND

The reaction of those left behind when someone emigrates depends on the relationship they have with the migrant. Feelings of loss and abandonment are inevitable. The one who stays behind may even experience feelings of hostility toward those who left. Depressive feelings and sorrow become more acute if it is known that this separation will be prolonged or permanent. Their feelings of mourning can be compared to those of people who have lost a loved one. The one who leaves dies, and so does the one who stays.[21] Not being able to be with my family physically for more than twenty years created a very deep relational emptiness. The family dynamic between my siblings is very basic and very occasional. We can feel as if we are literally strangers; they know very little about my life and I know very little about their lives. For them, I am the stranger, the one who walked away. They respect me because I am the oldest, but they don't trust me because they don't know me. My feelings of guilt and abandonment are no longer there because I was able to reunite with them; however, the breakup that our family relationship suffered is difficult to assimilate and repair.

LOSS AND BEREAVEMENT

Immigrants may initially grieve the loss of their native land, which greatly affects their self-esteem. Depending on their family background, they will gradually recover from this depression and accept their new environment and perhaps develop a sense of belonging. This adjustment to the new environment will depend on the individual's ability to cope with changes.[22] From a psychological point of view, migrating affects the person because this action implies leaving *the known life* and even part of one's identity to join a new model of life. Migratory grief is a process that is generated because of losses related to changing city or country of origin, regardless of whether the migration has been by choice or not. In all cases, it implies a significant adaptation to a new reality. Generally, we tend to believe that grief occurs only in the actual death of a person, but we also grieve other losses such as the breakup of a relationship, friendships, loss of a job or project, having to move to another city or country, or other losses. The difference between grief for the death of a loved one and grief for a migrant's losses is that in the latter case it is a multiple, partial, and recurrent grief. No other grief generates as many changes as migratory grief because it changes everything that surrounds the person who migrates. Migratory grief is *multiple* because the losses are several and diverse: language, interpersonal relationships such as family, friendships, the culture and traditions, the land, landscapes, seasons of the year, status in society, and contact with a group of belonging. Migratory grief is *partial* because what is lost does not disappear forever; it can be found again. This generates a strong emotional ambivalence. And it is *recurrent* because this possibility of returning to the place of origin of a visit, for example, can reactivate grief. Migratory grief is a normal and necessary psychological process that must be carried out effectively to avoid complications. The function of grief is to allow us to adapt to a new reality by accepting what we have lost.

The symptoms of migratory grief depend on how migration affects you psychologically. These symptoms are usually anxiety, depression, adaptation problems, increased stress, lack of appetite, insomnia, apathy, discouragement, psychosomatic diseases, and difficulties associated with identity and self-esteem. In the many meetings I have had with families who have recently arrived in this country, one of the most common moments is seeing them cry because of how difficult it is for them to live away from their families. Many of them had never been separated from their families, and now that they are not around, they experience everything described in this section on different levels.

CULTURE SHOCK

The insecure feelings that newly arrived immigrants experience arise not only from uncertainty and anxiety in the face of the unfamiliar but also the unavoidable regression that goes hand in hand with these anxieties. It is this regression that makes the immigrant feel unprotected and constrained at times, powerless to make use of the resources they have. These defense mechanisms are unconscious strategies that the immigrant uses to protect themselves from anxious thoughts or feelings. The displaced need a trustworthy person or community to help neutralize the fears or anxieties they feel toward the unknown or new culture. The need to feel welcome is such that any person or community who shows interest and behaves cordial and sympathetic will make the displaced loved.[23]

This state of regression is a natural reaction to the feelings of helplessness the displaced meet in this new environment. This includes disappointment in the reality of a new environment that differs from the initial ideological motivation that fueled the idea to emigrate, difficulties learning the new language, or the loss of their professional status.[24] In many cases, immigrants make the decision to immigrate to a specific country based on familiar or cultural connections to facilitate employment.[25]

A couple of months ago, in one of my conversations with a man who had recently arrived in the country, I asked him why he has not been able to look for a job, and his answer surprised me. He told me that he was very insecure because he was scared to speak English in public and, in attempting it, not being understood, and not being able to communicate. He told me that in his country of origin he was bullied because he had problems learning how to speak when growing up, and that he didn't want to experience those feelings again now as an adult.

The way members of the new community respond to the arrival of immigrants will have diverse influences on how they settle or adapt. The native community also feels the impact of the newcomers; in a certain way their presence modifies the existing group organization. Both the displaced and the native community feel that their identity is being threatened. Newcomers can approach the native community if this community shows respect for their dignity. The hostility of the new community can be manifested in the refusal to attempt to communicate with the foreign. Accentuating linguistic differences only hinders the dynamics for the migrants to feel adaptable in their new surroundings. The interaction between the newcomer and the native community must have a balance that allows both to participate in the process of getting to know each other in order to achieve a gradual integration of each of the parties.[26]

VIOLENCE

In many Latin American countries, violence is an everyday experience. Some Latin American cities are listed as the most violent in the world. Understanding the extent to which violence affects the immigrant is key to ministering and healing their hearts and minds. The types of violence that immigrants suffer can be divided into three categories: the violence experienced in their community of origin, the violence experienced on their journey to this country, and the violence of their reception in the United States.

It is no secret to anyone that Latin American countries experience incredible levels of violence. The Mexican government recently arrested one of the sons of the well-known drug trafficker Joaquín "El Chapo" Guzman. The violent response was not long in coming; thousands of members of the cartel came out and took over an entire city. They burned cars, blocked roads, shot at commercial planes, and innocent people were caught in the confrontations between government agents and cartel members. The cartel threatened the government that they would start killing hostages if they didn't release "El Raton" within seventy-two hours. That is just one example of the type of violence that is sadly experienced in most of this region. In a 2019 report, "four of the five most dangerous cities in the world are in Mexico. Fifteen Mexican cities made the list altogether. Latin America has an additional twenty-seven cities on the list."[27]

The drug trafficking and corruption in Mexico are the daily bread for residents in that country. The battles for the territory of the many drug cartels create very bloody episodes in many places. In addition to that, kidnappings, assaults, rapes, extortions, and disappearances happen at very high levels. Likewise, the countries of the so-called Northern Triangle face critical security concerns beyond the murder rate. Law enforcement is ineffective at providing protection; estimates show that 95 percent of the crimes go unpunished and only 3 percent of the murders are solved. Seeing that security systems cannot control violence, or that some of these systems are associated with cartels, gangs, or other crime organizations, forces the citizens choose not to report the violence and instead seek to leave their homeland. "People fleeing from violence experience significant mental health problems, including trauma-related disorders, depression, anxiety, substance abuse, and comorbidities between these diagnoses."[28]

Migrants who decide to leave their communities and embark on their journey to the United States face difficulties and violence, and many may even lose their lives. However, we need to understand that the challenges Mexican migrants face and the challenges Central American migrants face are different. Central American migrants must cross Mexico to arrive in the United States. Evidence suggests that migrants with fewer economic resources have the option of traveling by train (La Bestia). Those who have a little more capital can do it by bus or private car. Robbery, kidnapping, and assault are reportedly widespread. Female migrants face significant risk of sexual assault or sexual violence.

One of the most dangerous places to cross into the United States is the desert. The extreme temperatures can be deadly. In 2012, 463 bodies were found in the desert. The extreme condition of the desert makes bodies decompose faster, which often means that the corpses are not identified, and because of that their families never find them.[29] The migrants put their lives in the hands of hired *coyotes*, since they do not know the places or the routes to cross. They are disoriented and exposed to harsh conditions, and they are in danger of being taken advantage of by anyone.

My migratory journey was not the most pleasant. I remember leaving my homeland, saying goodbye to my mother and my sisters, who at the time were little girls. My uncles, a cousin, and I boarded a bus, and it took us three days to get to Tijuana. On the way I experienced discrimination in my own country. The security agents got us out of the bus, asked us to provide our documentation, and when they found out that we were going to Tijuana, they asked us for money to let us pass one of the checkpoints. It was the first time I experienced corruption and discrimination in my country. I was fifteen years old.

We arrived in Tijuana, rented a hotel, and the next day we moved to the place where we were going to cross into the United States. And so, with my backpack containing two changes of clothes, canned food, and a gallon of water in hand, we began to move away from the town to enter the hills. We waited until the afternoon to move a little further toward our first destination. Our first night in the hills was very cold, to the point that I remember my teeth were chattering from the cold. We walked for long hours and then rested. On many occasions we had to wait for the right moment to move forward.

I remember that some nights we could not sleep because it was raining very hard. On those nights we had to use plastic bags to cover ourselves and stand close to the trees or sit close to the rocks to avoid getting wet. Other nights I remember that we would walk and listen to the rattlesnakes near us. Honestly, I just waited for the moment when we accidentally stepped on the snakes, got bitten, and died. Some other nights we heard the coyotes howling. They were so close to us that I was scared. You find yourself so vulnerable to anything. I remember that some of the group could no longer continue, and they were left in the middle of the mountains.

I remember that when the border patrol detained us and took us to the detention center, we were sent back to Tijuana that same day. However, one of my uncles was imprisoned for three months. When we asked him why he was detained, he said that he had been told that one of us had identified him as our *coyote*. After investigating this among the four of us, we realized that no one identified my uncle as the *coyote*. What we believe is that they just wrongly accused him. My uncle mentioned that he will never forget those three months, because they treated him in a much-dehumanized way.

Unfortunately, there is a history of rhetorical violence against migrants in the United States. What is more worrying is that the Trump administrations have unleashed an even greater permissive discourse that is harmful to the immigrant community. There is an intimate connection between the rhetoric of hate and the violence itself.[30] We also need to consider that US immigration policy enacts violence against migrants from Mexico and Latin America as it persecutes, dehumanizes, and punishes them. Immigration detention itself has negative psychological consequences that worsen with the length of detention. For many, it triggers feelings of powerlessness, helplessness, uncertainty about the future, isolation, and fear about the safety of loved ones. The act of being criminalized can trigger the traumatic events that caused them to flee their homeland in the first place. Criminalizing migrants effectively tells them that they are what they have fled. The impact of criminalization can be understood clearly as violent.[31]

The electronic ankle monitor is one of the tools that the government uses to track immigrants and control their lives. I have met and talked with some people who have had to wear these devices. I asked them how they feel wearing them. Their answers have been very surprising. The most common responses are astonishment, since many of them do not fully understand why they must wear them: "I am not a criminal, I am here asking for asylum." "I'm being watched all the time." "I don't feel free." "I haven't done anything wrong." Many of them live in shame and depression for having to wear these devices. Other responses reflect the discomfort of wearing these devices: "I can't put on my pants." "I can't wear boots." "My foot hurts because of this device I have on." "I have marks on my skin, and it itches." All of them show their disagreement with comments like, "I'm desperate because of wearing this." "I'm going to cut the foot." "I'm going to break this freaking thing."

A few months ago, as part of a Justice and Mercy initiative in the church we planted, I had the opportunity to have a session with a couple from Colombia who had just arrived asking for asylum. They were newlyweds and had fled from Colombia because of the guerrilla groups. In the process of requesting asylum, they were separated and left in the detention center for a long period of time. The husband left the detention center first, but the wife was kept longer. When I asked the wife what had hurt the most during that experience, with tears in her eyes she replied, "I don't know why they had to handcuff me, I'm not a criminal, I've behaved well all my life, I did not deserve the treatment they gave me."

Seeking safety in the United States via asylum is, itself, a prolonged trauma. The backlog of these cases means that individuals may wait years for their cases to be adjudicated. Plus, the process is difficult and expensive.[32]

PSYCHIATRIC DISORDERS

This refers to a range of problems affecting the way individuals think, feel, and behave. Stressful life events can be precursors of psychiatric disorders. It is likely that those refugees whose migration has been associated with death of family members, loss of possessions, or threats to the migrant's life would be more likely to suffer from such disorders. Both migrants and refugees experience loss of social support caused by separation from the wider family network. Loss of social support is widely known to be a risk factor for the development of serious mental disorders. The following factors can lead to psychological disorders among migrants and refugees: events or conditions leading up to the decision to migrate or flee; loss of family, possessions left behind, dangers on the journey; conditions upon arrival in a host community; culture shock; lack of family or other social support; difficult living conditions; continued worries concerning family members left behind; and discrimination by the host community.[33]

The immigrant can also experience what is known as an acute stress reaction. This is something individuals may develop after a particularly stressful event, whether physical or mental. The stressor may be an overwhelming traumatic experience involving a serious threat to the security or physical integrity of the subject or loved one, as in natural catastrophes, accidents, criminal assaults, rapes, or an unusually sudden change in the social position or network of the individual. The symptoms may include withdrawal from expected social interaction, narrowing of attention, apparent disorientation, anger or verbal aggression, despair or hopelessness, or uncontrollable and excessive grief.[34] Acute stress disorder is different from PTSD because of the symptoms typically last only three days to one month after the exposure of the traumatic event.[35]

PTSD is another disorder that the displaced person might experience. As previously discussed, it arises as a delayed or protracted response to a stressful event or situation. The onset of PTSD follows the trauma with a latency period that may range from a few weeks to months but rarely exceeds six months. The symptoms include persistent remembering or reliving of the stressor by intrusive flashbacks, vivid memories, recurring dreams, or by experiencing distress when exposed to circumstances resembling or associated with the stressor.[36] The *Diagnostic and Statistical Manual of Mental Disorders* underlines the following when addressing PTSD: directly experiencing any traumatic event; recurrent, involuntary, and intrusive distressing memories of the traumatic event; flashbacks in which the individual feels or acts as if the traumatic event was recurring; or avoidance of or efforts to avoid distressing memories or external reminders of the traumatic event. The individual can also experience dissociative symptoms such as depersonalization, persistent or recurrent feelings of detachment, as if one were an outside observer or derealization, or feelings of a sense of unreality that is dreamlike or distant. The duration of the symptoms varies; while some may recover within months, other individuals remain symptomatic for over twelve months, and sometimes for more than fifty years.[37]

Post-traumatic stress disorder can disrupt your entire life: your work, your interpersonal relationships, your health, and your satisfaction with daily activities. Having PTSD also increases your risk of other mental health problems, such as depression and anxiety, problems with drug and alcohol use, eating disorders, and suicidal thoughts and actions.

TRAUMA

Trauma changes the way people look at themselves, and most importantly, can cause long term behavioral and personality changes. Trauma can have significant impact on our soul; in fact, *trauma* is the Greek word that means injury to the soul. Trauma shatters one's sense of feeling safe. It can also disrupt our belief system and alter our views about a loving creator, so there is a correlation between trauma and an individual's spiritual wellness.[38] It limits and damages the ability to regulate our emotions. Situations that other people can tolerate become intolerable to us. Many times, without any reason or apparent warning, we feel worried, irritated, distressed, depressed, scared, or even all of these feelings at the same time, without being able to do anything about it. We seem to navigate between intensity and numbness, or anxiety and numbness, unable to find a middle ground. We find it very difficult to calm down on our own, to feel calm, or to seek and accept help from others. Trauma results in fragmentation and dissociation within us. This occurs, for example, when we suppress parts of what happened to us from our memory, when we remember all the details but feel nothing in the face of the horror of the memory, or when entire parts of our personality remain closed off and absent after the traumatic event. In some cases, symptoms might be well understood with an anxiety- or fear-based context. Trauma and stress related disorders are intimately related with attachment disorder, disinhibited social engagement disorder, post-traumatic stress disorder, acute stress disorder, adjustment disorder, and prolonged grief disorder.[39]

LETTER FROM A TRAUMATIZED IMMIGRANT

While working on this chapter, I couldn't help but remember myself as that fifteen-year-old boy. Today my pain and suffering make more sense. The questions of why I feel the way I feel, or why those things happened to me; became clearer. I look through the pages of my story: the mornings when I woke up and thought it was all a dream, and the afternoons when I cried inconsolably for being away from my family and my homeland. The pain of not being able to hug my loved ones; the moments when I longed with all the strength of my being for a kiss, a hug, a word of encouragement.

I remember feeling incomplete and expressing that feeling by screaming and crying, which caused many sleepless nights. I remember the times when people spoke to me and I couldn't answer them out of sadness, and I wondered why it was so difficult for me to relate to others. The times I walked through the streets without thinking, without focus, looking at the cars passing by on the freeways with the desire to throw myself in the road so as not to feel that emptiness.

The times I felt incapable of being able to do something. The feeling of failure when trying to speak in English. It still hurts not to have a connection with my siblings, not to have memories of growing up together. The fear of entering a place where Spanish was not spoken so as not to feel embarrassed for not speaking English. The fear of being deported even if you are far from a place of detention.

I diagnosed myself and realized that I am broken, incomplete. It has been twenty-four years, and it still hurts like it was yesterday. Oh my God! It still hurts to not be from this place, nor the place where I was born. It hurts not to have been able to find someone who would help me, who would care about me, who would look beyond appearances. It hurts to know that there are thousands who suffer today just like me. It hurts because I know what it feels like.

THE GOOD NEWS BRINGS HEALING

A journey of faith with God in the form of a personal relationship can heal and restore the wounds of our soul. This relationship can be an effective coping mechanism, and trauma survivors who have faith have gained more optimistic perspectives and found greater meaning and purpose for their experiences.[40] Congregations or faith communities are the primary instrument of granting Christian identity. They provide a sense of community, especially in times of crisis; they establish social links; they nurture an ethic of service; and can change narratives based on God's story.[41]

Churches function as agents of the good news embracing a mission not bound by geographical, social, economic, racial, ethnic, cultural, or political borders. The church can be a community of compassion, a dwelling place of the healing Spirit, the incarnated body of Jesus walking among the marginalized. It can be a holistic place for a new creation, a new society of freedom, justice, peace, respect, and equality.

We often forget the power that emanates from each place that is consecrated as a church. The power of a community of faith can restore, heal, guide, and empower the displaced who have lost not only their dignity and identity, but everything that was familiar to them. The incredible mystery about the church is that it is not tied to a location or building; the church can exist and be in any space, even in the most unexpected of places. In times when the migration phenomenon has intensified due to different situations in the world, let us be the church that walks together with the displaced.

CHAPTER FOUR

Pastoral Care in the Margins

In one of my last classes at Fuller I had the opportunity to explore deeper into the segregation that was experienced in the United States until the late '60s. For me, it was shocking to read and see the painful and excruciating reality that was experienced for the African American community at that time. I got goose bumps, and my heart cried when I saw that an area or space was divided, limited to use based on skin color. Two realities were lived in the same area or space: on the one hand, the dominant culture, the privileged, and on the other, the marginalized. When it comes to migration, the displaced live segregated, not due only to skin color, but rather, due to the lack of documents that prove their legality in the country, due to the inability to speak English, or due to lack of knowledge of the new culture. During the civil rights movement, there were many who raised their voices so that others could see the change in attitude that was needed in relation to racial differences. Currently, it is necessary to continue pointing out the need we have to adapt immigration policy to the new reality of this country. Pastoral work becomes the helm that will take the local church to those horizons.

This chapter is dedicated to those who do ministry on the margins in any part of the world. The reality that exists regarding immigration in this nation is a reality parallel to many other countries. Thank you for accepting the call to go places where not everyone wants to go. As for those who God has called to work and serve immigrants, thank you for doing a job that is very demanding, and often little recognized. Thank you for not closing your eyes to a reality so visible, yet so ignored. Thank you for being the visible love of God, in places invisible to many, but where God orchestrates his plans to expand his kingdom. Thank you for embodying mercy and justice to provide dignity to a community that has lost it due to bureaucratic policies.

NEW PASTORAL DIMENSIONS

Pastoral work on the margins of society represents a challenge in many dimensions of an already very demanding vocation. On the margins, the individual aspect of pastoral work takes on very different features from the image that was held of the pastor a few decades ago. The image of a pastor sitting in their office attending to the needs of the people who attend church is not the dynamic of ministry on the margins. In fact, pastoral care now involves many other aspects that previously did not appear in the pastor's curriculum. When we talk specifically about the margins of society, we are talking about how this community represents a challenge due to its enormous physical, psychological, and spiritual need.[1]

Ministry in the margins has to do with living beyond the immediate, always facing dystopian realities. The more you dive into the depths of the margins, the more your heart is constricted by the enormous need you find. It is a very challenging and dangerous vocation, and in many cases, this work goes unnoticed. It is a calling that demands too much and that puts you in front of very complex situations. Suffering, danger, and poverty; these are elements that accompany many ignored communities that walk on the margins. It is not a call about power or control, but a call to live in powerlessness and humility; not because of weakness or passivity, but because these pastors abandon their power in favor of the manifestation of God's love, humble to obey wherever God leads them.[2]

On top of that, in the margins, you are faced with many ethical and legal dilemmas. For example, in Florida, on July 1, 2024, a law signed by Governor Ron DeSantis came into effect that makes life difficult for undocumented immigrants in the state and that establishes harsh penalties not only for those who employ them, but even for those who transport them in their vehicles. Those who transport undocumented immigrants could be charged with a felony. Another example is that job applicants often need to present "valid" documentation and undocumented immigrants then come to the pastor asking for advice on how to obtain that documentation. A few months ago, I had the opportunity to go to Ensenada, Mexico to assist a ministry in that city. While we were walking through the streets of the city, the person who was guiding me, who was also originally from there, pointed me to a church. He told me, "The pastor of this church died preaching in the pulpit." I was intrigued by what he told me, so I asked him to give me more details. Apparently, in that neighborhood there were people involved in organized crime, and in some way or another in his role as pastor this man got in their way; they ended up killing him. A group of gunmen arrived and killed him one Sunday morning when he was preaching.

A few years ago, another young minor arrived in Tijuana with no one to help him. The young man approached a church in the 20 de Noviembre neighborhood there in Tijuana; he got closer to God and joined the church, but he made the decision to try to cross over to the United States. Having no one to help him, being a minor and having no one to watch over him, the pastor of the church decided to be the one to negotiate the deal with the *coyote* so that the young man could cross the border. The pastor took him to the place where the *coyote* would meet them. He knew where they were hiding and how dangerous that journey was. The young man arrived in the United States and is still in contact with the pastor who helped him. These are just a couple of examples of the ethical and legal complexities of pastoring on the margins.

For the pastor, the margins are a call to model hospitality. This is very difficult in an individualistic and egocentric society. Hospitality is the ability to pay attention to the guest. For us to pay attention to the guest, our soul must be at rest. If we want to achieve this, it is necessary to precondition our heart by living in concentration, meditation, contemplation, and silence. When we manage to be at peace with ourselves, then we can be hospitable to a guest who needs to feel at home, in confidence, and among family.[3] Hospitality in the margins is about releasing the seed of creativity to find the most effective way to show God's love transforming lives. It involves investing our energy and gifts in service to others, hoping for a new horizon for those who live complex realities. It is a vocation based on justice and compassion. It is a place where you learn to perceive or see God in each guest who is looking for a better life. Mark Deymaz uses a very interesting term to describe the contemporary pastor: disruptive innovator. The disrupter operates outside conventional wisdom, turning systems upside down to effect systemic change. They first define, then refine, and ultimately create new realities by changing the way we see things. They frame questions, shape the narrative, and influence the conversation. They lead us to see things differently, to think differently, and to do things differently.[4] To change realities it is often necessary to navigate against the existing; that is a risk that those who work on the margins must take into account.

The pastor in the margins must be prepared to face some of the same obstacles or problems the marginalized experience. They too can suffer from feelings of discrimination, racism, and xenophobia. Events like these can lead to traumatic experiences. It is also important that these pastors become aware of unacknowledged or unresolved traumas in their own history, since these personal traumas can impede a minister's capacity to deal with trauma in the lives of others.[5] To prevent this from becoming an obstacle, the pastor needs to be grounded in the spiritual reality of belonging to God. The pastor is God's beloved. As the beloved, they can oppose, comfort, rebuke, and encourage without fear of rejection or need of affirmation. They can experience persecution but have no desires for revenge. They can give everything without expecting anything in return. They live freely, without borders and without affiliations that cause them to stay quiet when the truth must be told.[6]

Due to the complexity of the context of the margins, discernment becomes a main element. The concept of immigration as *waves* perfectly describes the dynamics of those who minister in this context. The pastor in immigrant churches ministers a community that is passing through, in movement, in a process of starting and establishing a life in a new country. Perhaps, the pastor's interaction with a certain family or individual will consist of a single meeting, or it may require them to accompany the migrant through an asylum or deportation process. Perhaps, the pastor will accompany a person until they fix their immigration situation; it could be a month, or ten years. Discernment discovers and affirms the unique way God's love and direction are manifested for a specific purpose, so we can know God's will and fulfill his calling and mission within the community we pastor. Discernment will help us have a divine perspective to position or guide each wave of immigrants to the will of God. Therefore, discernment calls us to settle into God's ways of measuring time, handling specific situations, and acting in each encounter. The dystopia on the margins can become a burden if we do not learn to rest in the *kairos* of God. *Kairos* has to do with opportunities, moments, situations that are ripe for an intended purpose. The *kairos* contains the past, present, and future of the trajectory of those who experience a migratory journey.[7]

NEW ECCLESIASTICAL DIMENSIONS

One dilemma we face is the demand to develop more realistic pastoral responses for migrants. It is time to reflect on our ecclesiastical models and adjust them to a new reality. The revival that is happening in the Hispanic context should be an inspiration for all of us as we reflect on providing pastoral care for migrants. For the church, acknowledging this reality means a commitment to getting in touch with the Hispanic existence. The Hispanic people are here, and there are more coming. With the crisis at the border the church is being challenged as never before to offer a more comprehensive pastoral response to the Hispanic reality of our time.[8]

For this, there has to be a comprehensive understanding of the needs and realities of this community and the new ecclesiastical dimensions that pastoral work implies. Therefore, it is necessary to understand that the Hispanic community is already part of the American church. We can no longer unrealistically picture that Hispanics are the church of yesterday or tomorrow, because the clear reality is that they are the church of today. It is necessary to be more conscious of the Hispanic presence. Many well-intentioned pastors do not realize how many Hispanics are living in their neighborhood surroundings. Becoming sensitive to the increasing presence of the displaced community can make the transition to a multicultural world easier, although such transition is inevitably chaotic and arduous at times. However, refusing this reality will make matters even more challenging in the end and generate many different and unresolved tensions.[9]

The ecclesiastical dimension at the margins involves true hospitality that is both real and welcoming to the displaced. We have often heard the very beautiful call to "open wide the doors." This refrain is subject to a variety of interpretations on many different and important levels, but part of the implication deals with the pastoral care of immigrants. More than simply a catchy motto, the theme of opening wide the doors has many implications for the host. Yet opening these doors is a decision for mission, not only to benefit migrants but the entire American church. At the very minimum an open church is a church without borders. If we do not remove the idea of hospitality as a task to be accomplished, that we must provide, then we stay in a position of power. Real hospitality goes further; it leads us to share what is ours so that it belongs to both of us.[10] For example, in Southern California, Pastor Melvin Valiente and his wife decided that their church would be a sanctuary for immigrants facing deportation. The First Baptist Church of Maywood on East 57th Street in Los Angeles was one of the first to show this gesture of hospitality in response to the terrible reality faced by families who were going to be affected by the announcement of massive raids.[11]

Many of our pastoral models are conditioned to our weekly activities: a Sunday service, Bible study, and a prayer session. We have unconsciously formed restrictions that limit contact with the reality of the community to which we minister. In my experience over the years, it has become increasingly clear to me that the biggest borders that need to be crossed are not the borders of countries but the borders of our own hearts. In this context, the hospitality we must embody needs to go beyond mere lip service and become as real and as welcoming as possible. By breaking down the barriers and opening all the doors of our local churches, immigrants can make our church into something new. Pastoral care on the margins means providing spaces and places for individuals to feel welcome and to practice their faith.[12]

New ecclesiastic models must realize that pastoral counseling takes on another dimension at the margins. It's not an office job. The church of the margins must adapt to all types of conditions and locations.[13] The displaced person experiences so many shortcomings that the pastor must be ready to advise at anytime, anywhere. It could be in the hotel where a family newly arrived in the country is staying, or in the detention center. It could be at the park, or at a restaurant because the family needed to have a meal, or at any social agency, on street corners, or any unconventional place. Private or uninterrupted spaces are often not available for a counseling session at the margins.

New ecclesiastic models need an approach of integration that emphasizes the virtues of welcoming. The pastoral care of migrants means welcome, respect, protection, promotion, and genuine love of every person in their religious and cultural expressions. The local church needs to be committed to sparing no effort in developing a strategy among this community to help them settle in their new context and to foster a welcoming attitude of openness and brotherhood. Welcoming immigrants requires acts like the creation of free spaces where the stranger can enter and become a friend instead of an enemy. Welcoming immigrants does not mean to change people, but to offer them space where change can take place. It is not to bring people over to our side, but to offer freedom not disturbed by divisive lines.[14]

New ecclesiastic models need to recognize the importance of culture in seeking to integrate immigrants into the economic, social, civil, and political spheres as much as possible. The immigrant community searches for a place that provides a sense of identity and dignity. One of the common traits discovered in this community has been a very low self-esteem, and a very modest self-image.[15] Culture includes the values of a given people, and the relationship between faith or religion and culture merits particular attention. Historically, religion has played a key role in forming the values of its followers. Religious institutions can provide social belonging, psychological comfort, and religious meaning, so migrants can enter a space that is familiar. Culture is neither motionless, nor endlessly flexible. It shifts from one generation to the next, and throughout a lifetime. As the culture of the strangers begin to influence the culture of a host community, both strangers and host often find themselves in unfamiliar and often uncomfortable positions.[16] Pastoral work involves mediating and conciliating between different groups and cultures in a specific context.

A church at the margins should expect to use different methods than those used for people who are born in the United States or those who have assimilated the new culture. Goals borrowed from psychotherapy such as growth through self-awareness, personality integration through resolving inner conflicts, and movement toward self-fulfillment are goals that must wait, not because they are not valid goals, but because the displaced person is dealing with other realities. For example, I currently pastor a family that, because of their migratory journey and how difficult it has been for them to adapt to their new life, have experienced tensions in the relationship and interactions between husband and wife that have brought them to the point of wanting to separate. There is another family where the husband has to work nights to make more money because his wife's health is not stable, and he needs to generate more income to cover the expenses here in the United States and those they have in their country of origin. As a result, the husband has suffered a change in his character that makes communication with his wife very complex, creating continuous conflicts between them. There is another family that broke relationships with relatives living in this country because in their opinion they did not help them like a family does in Latin America, where everyone helps each other within a family. Although many of the conditions and outcomes are the same as any relationship in crisis, the difference is that these cases have their roots in the family's immigration experience; therefore, the approach must be different.

The church at the margins should establish methods and goals based first on the circumstance of the person or family. It is important to remember that we will not be able to develop a prescriptive methodology that will work with all immigrant families, therefore, it is important that the counselor adopt a method with cultural sensibility that is trauma informed, and that they understand the dynamics and effects of migration on people.

The church must position itself at the level of understanding the reality of each case or scenario. They should practice more action-oriented methods, focused on the basic needs of the moment and with short-term goals that understand the lack of assimilation to the new culture. Above all, these methods should involve accompaniment as an essential component.[17] The church needs to study these factors in order to understand this community better and to design more effective strategies for outreach, discipleship, church founding, and church growth.[18]

Another challenge for ecclesiastical models in the immigrant church is language and understanding generational differences, in this case among Hispanics. There are notable differences between generations. The church must be aware of what stage of assimilation the different members are in. An ideal situation will be when the congregation is at the same level of assimilation and have similar understandings with regard to culture, leadership styles, and organizational patterns.[19]

NEW STRUCTURES

About a decade ago, when I was studying at the faculty of theology, a teacher mentioned that the days when people came to the church building were over. For him, the church now needed to go out of building and bring the church to the people. Now the church is no longer defined by a building. The Sunday School movement formally began in Britain in the 1780s. Soon the movement spread to North America, as well. Denominations and nondenominational organizations caught the vision and energetically began creating Sunday schools. Within decades the movement had become extremely popular. By the mid-nineteenth century, Sunday school attendance was a nearly universal aspect of the church. Even parents who did not attend church regularly usually insisted that their children go to Sunday school. Over several decades, however, this model of doing church has gradually disappeared, and since then there has not been an efficient model for creating disciples.

Historically, the success of the spread of the gospel has depended on the fantastic ability of the church to adapt to the contextual reality of the changing times. In this case, the immigrant community needs other ecclesiastical elements to carry out an integral mission. The reality of the displaced community challenges us to create new ecclesiastical models, very different from the current ones. For example, in New York City, many churches, including St. John's Episcopal Church, have chosen to give their properties a different use. In this case, the church is pursuing the potential of a fifty-seven-bed asylum-seeker shelter. The church considers it its moral obligation to help the displaced in this way. Despite opposition, the church said it has a moral and ethical obligation to help those in crisis.[20]

In California, the SB4 law, or as some call it "Yes in God's Backyard" allows affordable housing projects on property owned by churches or other religious institutions to bypass an extensive review process and be able to build multi-family homes. It is also a reality that some of these churches are facing revenue shortfalls. Therefore, getting into housing may be a way for them to find new purpose and new sources of revenue.²¹ Another interesting case is that of the Evangelical Alliance for Immigration Services. Its founder, Steve Sanford, wanted to provide family-based immigration services for people who needed to confirm legal status, reunite with loved ones, and strengthen immigrant families, and he set up an office inside the Mosaic church facilities. Since its foundation it has helped the Hispanic community in Arkansas.²²

Within the multiple needs faced by the displaced community, step by step, different ministries may emerge to focus on some of these aspects: for example, how to help immigrants take steps toward citizenship or how to help them obtain health care services. These ministries are giving a new structure to the church; it is no longer just a Sunday service and a Bible study, but now we must look for ways to make the church present among immigrants.

ELEMENT OF JUSTICE

Historically, immigrants are labeled with different adjectives that denigrate their dignity and value as a creation in the image of God. I believe President Trump's statements in 2016 are a clear example of this. Referring to immigrants as "criminals" denigrates and generalizes an entire community. Therefore, it is important to understand that pastoring on the margins implies keeping this aspect of justice in mind, not only because of historical reality, but because of our human tendency to denigrate God's image in others.

The Hebrew word for justice is *mishpat*. This word puts emphasis on the action. The word *mishpat* occurs more than four hundred times in the Old Testament. The basic meaning of *mishpat* is to treat people equitably or in an impartial manner; abstractly, it refers to justice, including a participant's right or privilege. In Leviticus 24:22, *mishpat* means acquitting or punishing every person on the merits of the case, regardless of race or social status. On the other hand, it also means to give people their rights.²³ Justice in practical life is expressed in caring for the most vulnerable. Biblical narrative often presents God as the defender of the vulnerable (Deut 10:17–18). In Hebrew the words that are translated as *righteousness* and *justice* (*sedeqah* and *mishpat*) and their derivatives are often used together or interchangeably. Both have to do with living justly and according to God's purposes, a rightness in relationships, a wholeness to life for the individual and the community. In his discussion of three related aspects of liberation, the Latin American theologian Gustavo Gutiérrez helps us see that our work for justice, our friendships and our personal righteousness are interrelated parts of God's work of salvation or healing. He describes: (1) social liberation from structural evil and exploitation—changing the political and economic structures that keep some people from life and freedom, (2) personal liberation—the freedom that comes with sharing life in community, building relationships, experiencing respect and telling stories of a different kind of world that is possible, and (3) spiritual liberation from personal sin that comes with salvation and sanctification in Christ.[24]

The social programs or initiatives that we have in the church have the purpose of proclaiming the dignity and value that each person possesses before God. This arises from the reality experienced by displaced people who are constantly mistreated as if they have no value. In fact, the approach that our ministry acquired was thanks to Manna SoCal. The process of thinking about an initiative to bless our community was what confirmed the focus that we have as a church today. Founder James Gann was the one who taught us to do church in a different way. This element of justice is vitally important to embrace a community that needs to recuperate a sense of belonging and identity. Our initiative aims to change the narrative of pain, suffering, and unworthiness to one of joy, empowerment and purpose for the displaced.

Our program consists of five lessons that enable us to "Keep on Walking":

1. Abraham's calling—A movement with purpose
2. Joseph's story—Changing our narrative from suffering to fullness

3. The exodus—A new land, a new story
4. Psalm 139 and Genesis 1:27—Recovering your value and identity
5. Jeremiah 29, the exiles—Being a good citizen and a good Christian

The five lessons that make up our initiative have the purpose of creating safe spaces and, through biblical stories, finding parallels with the stories of immigrant families. Within these sessions we provide a safe space for families to assimilate their experiences, but also to allow God to heal all unpleasant events. These stories show us how God is always using movement to create something new, and they learn that their arrival in this country is only part of that movement of God. We invite them to let God change their stories of pain and hopelessness for stories of purpose and abundance. Also, financial support is provided, and church families are always willing to help in any way they can.

ECONOMIC ELEMENTS

When I first started working as an assistant pastor for a Hispanic ministry in an English-speaking church. I remember one Sunday, a few minutes after the service ended that morning, a Hispanic man arrived at the door of the church. He knocked on the door and I answered. When I opened the door, before he started to speak, I saw that he had a flyer in his hand. This man introduced himself in Spanish and proceeded to request help to bury his daughter because she had been murdered by a cartel in Mexico. The flyer in his hand showed pictures of his daughter, but also, some images of the crime scene. While the man was speaking with me, a lead pastor showed up and started listening to the man's request. When the man finished his request, the lead pastor asked the man to wait a few minutes to consider the request. We went to the lead pastor's office, and he decided not to help this man. The lead pastor was afraid of a scam. Before letting the man know our decision, the lead pastor asked my opinion about this situation. I responded that we should help the man, because his request seemed legitimate. The lead pastor's response was that the church's money was not used for that kind of request. I believe the lead pastor was not familiar with how people suffer from the effects of cartel violence.

Pastoral work on the margins confronts you with peoples' terrible financial need. Therefore, those who work on the margins will live in that constant tension between paying the operating expenses of the church and looking for ways to alleviate the financial burden that most immigrants face. It is not only the suffering, but also the scarcity, the limitations that usually accompany those who live on the margins. Hispanics and Blacks are among the poorest races in the United States,[25] although the poverty you experience in the United States does not compare to that of most Latin American countries. Also, first generation Hispanics who do not speak English are more likely to have low incomes and financial difficulties; they may even avoid using bank accounts. Therefore, it is important to develop a strong sense of stewardship.[26]

In our church's case, part of our monthly budget is allocated to help the family members of our faith community who we know are most in need. One of the stories that has marked our lives and ministry has been the story of a friend from Colombia. He is no longer with us; he died two years ago. Our friend started coming to church after the doctors declared him terminally ill, stating that he would live only for another six months. He had lung problems and had to be connected to an oxygen tank. Our friend had no family in California and lived alone, renting a room. We watched him grow in his faith with God and he became a pioneer of our ministry, but his health deteriorated to the point that he could no longer work. After our friend could no longer work, although he never gave up, he always tried to do something to generate an income and not feel useless, as he used to say; our friend struggled a lot to survive. His legal status did not allow him to apply to be admitted to a nursing home permanently, and he could not travel to Colombia because he permanently needed to be connected to the oxygen tank. Although his employer tried to help him, his health no longer allowed him to work. A church family set up a room for him to live in and helped him with the application to maintain his oxygen treatment through medical care. In the last months of his life the entire church helped him in one way or another: covering his expenses, cleaning his room, cooking for him, visiting him, and so on. In the moments when he most needed the church, we were there. When he died all of us cried. It was a very hard moment; we loved him very much.

In my last conversation with him, he thanked me for all the support as his spiritual family and told me that he was ready if God decided to take him. Seven years had passed from the moment he was declared permanently ill. In those seven years we were able to create an incredible relationship, but also, we learned how complicated it can be to not have the necessary financial resources. That is only one story of the pastoral reality with the displaced.

Currently, we are only leasing a meeting place, and no one receives a salary, as such; this makes it easier to cover operational expenses and prioritize the financial aspect of the neediest among us. Also, we have offered financial administration seminars or classes. These seminars offer different resources, from opening a bank account to the basic principles of a retirement plan. Our ministry has adopted a community economy; that is, we try to put Acts 4:32 into practice. Finances are used to cover operational expenses, to help needy church members, and to reach out to the community. Internally, we constantly have conversations with members to guide them in their finances; our goal is to guide them to be financially sustainable based on their situation.

FLEXIBLE NETWORKS

There are basic needs that the immigrant community often cannot cover, either because it does not have the financial capital to do so or because it does not know how to do so. Among these needs we find costs for the legal immigration process, the search for housing, and the search for a job. Daniel Sanchez provides a survey of Hispanic pastors that was conducted by the research department of the North American Mission Board. The survey found that the following needs of the Hispanic community were what the pastors considered most vital to assist this community:

1. Helping people to get jobs or better jobs: 68%
2. Helping new immigrants establish themselves: 60.8%
3. Helping persons to have a better access to basic social services: 60.8%
4. Counseling programs: 60.8%
5. English or citizenship classes: 58.3%
6. Helping students stay in school: 53.3%
7. Childcare programs: 45%
8. Food distribution: 37.5%
9. Adequate housing: 25.5%

The complexity in meeting or satisfying the needs of this community is enormous; however, good networking can help facilitate pastoral work.[27] The pastor needs to cultivate the concept of complementarity and mutual assistance between ministries rather than the feeling of competition with each other. For example, our ministry has expanded our network to be able to assist in meeting the needs of each family. We have established relationships with immigration lawyers or organizations that deal with immigration cases. We have a relationship with a non-profit organization focused on the family, offering family therapies including immigration issues. We have contacted employment agencies to have different options for those looking for a job. In my case, I have referred individuals as strong candidates for different open positions in different companies. We have gone to talk to apartment owners so that they give the opportunity to families who have no credit history but need housing. Also, I recently witnessed how Manna SoCal is trying to assist Hispanics by providing grants for small ministries. They have allowed me to share this news with fellow pastors, friends who live similar realities regarding immigration in their communities. We have learned to use the resources available and always be open to expanding our network. A few months ago, Dr. Alexia Salvatierra of Matthew 25, a nonprofit organization created to accompany, protect, and advocate for asylum seekers, told me: "Francisco, there is no need to walk alone; today we already have many resources at hand to help our communities."

DISCIPLESHIP IN THE MARGINS

Some ministries have decided not to have activities or meetings during the week because it is difficult for families or people to attend. On the margins, and especially within the immigrant community, discipleship becomes a challenge. This community lives with constant adjustments here in the United States. We must remember that historically, this community tends to have jobs not only less remunerated, but also with very complicated schedules. Some are trying to go to school to learn English, while others have two jobs to be able to cover the expenses of their families here and in their countries of origin.

During discipleship, we need to begin to encourage immigrants to be fully alive in their faith so that they can transition from being passive sheep to active shepherds in the community.[28] In our case, we have adopted a discipleship that incorporates the reality of the person after arriving in this country. We are very intentional about creating spaces to address issues such as losses due to migration. We understand that new immigrant believers experience many emotional burdens and financial challenges while pursuing stability. We have seen that family dynamics change, in addition to each member being affected in different ways. Also, immigrants are trying to understand the new culture. Therefore, it is a slow-paced discipleship, based on accompaniment and being attentive to their reality; providing biblical growth, but also giving room and openness to cultivate their faith based in their reality. We can say that our discipleship consists of five integral aspects that are addressed depending on the situation and reality of each believer (see Figure 4.1).

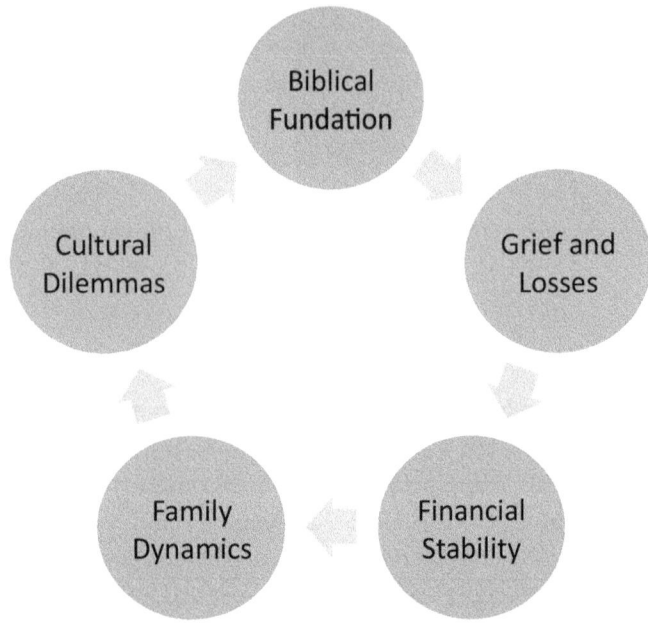

Figure 4.1. Sustainable discipleship in the margins.

We have been fortunate to see how the families who joined our ministry a few years ago and who have received this discipleship now offer themselves to accompany new families who arrive in this country and are living what they had to live through when they first arrived. These immigrant believers become active members in the community and continue healing a suffering community. Literally, they become wounded healers.

One of the aspects of discipleship that is crucial in the margins is that of the family. One of the serious mistakes that we often make is wanting to see disciples involved in all the activities of the church. However, we must never forget that in the establishment process in this country, families face excessive demands. It hurts us to see people involved in the church, but with families destroyed or neglected because of the church. Our recommendation for our ministry volunteers is that they always get involved in the church, but without affecting their interactions with their families.

LETTER FROM AN UNDOCUMENTED PASTOR

Dear ministry colleagues and church leaders. I hope God is pouring blessings on your life, family, and ministry. As you know, our undocumented status forces us to act with a low profile. Although we often go unnoticed, here we are in this great nation. Usually, we have small ministries in places we rent. Our ministries often carry nuances of our native countries or communities. Most of us are bi-vocational because our ministries alone cannot sustain us, and like Paul, we decided not to financially burden our congregation.

You already know how complicated and demanding the ministry is, therefore, you will understand when I tell you that it has been very difficult to respond to my call. Not only have I had to overcome my insecurities and identity problems due to my undocumented status, but I have also had to overcome the labels that society puts on you for not having legal documents. Furthermore, some have questioned my calling. Some have told me that my calling does not exist. Some others have called me criminal. Some have suggested me to ask God for forgiveness for having crossed illegally. Some others have ignored me, and I have suffered different treatment. It hasn't been easy, I had to navigate alone, but in the end, everything has worked for good.

Regarding my family, I can tell you that as a husband it has been very frustrating to see our marriage goals and dreams be stopped by my status. I still remember the many times we tried to buy a house but because of my situation, my income could not be considered. We needed the two incomes, especially in California where one income is not enough to buy a house unless you have a well-paying job. I also remember when, due to my condition, we could not go on vacation so as not to expose myself to being detained and deported. I remember my wife saying, let's go to San Diego, and me responding, no, because there is a border patrol check point in Temecula.

Despite all the limitations that I may have as an undocumented person and pastor, I am very happy with the way the gospel is flourishing in the Hispanic community, especially among new migrants. I have witnessed the power of God healing wounded hearts pursuing the desire to have a better life. I have had to pastor the undocumented, being undocumented myself. Sometimes in our meetings, we joke that *la migra* is going to come and we will face deportation, but in our hearts, we rest in the sovereignty of God, longing for the freedom we will enjoy one day.

We have wanted to have a building where we can meet; however, we have realized that many of our community members often cannot even afford their monthly rent because they are still working to have financial stability. So, we have given up on that idea, due to the reality we live in. However, we continue to yearn to have not only a meeting space, but also a place where the families of our community can live. At a conference I attended in Michigan, it was mentioned that a church had built apartments they could lease at a low cost, benefiting newly arrived migrant families but also helping the community to mitigate the weight of a very demanding economy. A ministerial model like that would be great for us! Because of that same reality I have had to give up some financial privileges that many other pastors have. But thank God, other doors have opened to be able to provide for my family and in this way allow the church to support more families.

I ask you to please continue praying, so that God continues to heal the wounded hearts of his people. May the sovereign God protect all the displaced he has brought with the purpose of continuing to build and expand his church in this country. May God continue to move the hearts of those in power to be able to welcome immigrant families and create an environment of hospitality towards strangers. May God continue to bless this great nation and continue to raise up his church. Amen.

Conclusion

The future of Christianity in the United States depends to a great extent on how we respond and develop the potential of Hispanic immigrants for the kingdom of God. We currently face an incredible pastoral challenge due to the complex way that the displaced arrive in this country. Our preparation, assimilation, and ecclesiastical creativity will determine the progress of the future church.

This pastoral work needs to incorporate elements that will bring us closer to this community that usually walks on the margins. Consequently, I suggest that we need to be preparing the local church on several levels to be active and proactive participants in the missionary activity that this community represents. We need to prepare leaders aware of their surroundings and the multiculturalism that surrounds them. We especially need leaders aware of the needs of the immigrant community so they can become active agents of evangelization in their neighborhoods.

We cannot be comfortable allowing these new Christians to stay in their *barrios*. Rather, we should equip them and empower them to use their gifts, talents, and unique faith expressions to transform the world in new and wonderful ways. For this, it is crucial to give Hispanic immigrants a space and place to feel at home. The only place or organization capable of providing dignity, love, and healing is the church, and our congregations need to be reminded of this biblical truth.

The act of walking with the immigrant community on their journey toward their new homeland where they will start a new season in their lives and a new Christian identity can be a reassuring way of serving them to preserve their faith in God. For the church, getting in touch with this reality means a commitment to getting in touch with the immigrant presence. While many feel threatened by this emerging immigrant presence, my own experience has proven over and over again that the presence of new immigrants is renewing our congregations and bringing new hope to our neighborhoods. However, this only becomes a reality when we are open to accepting the newcomer and work creatively, providing them with adequate pastoral care. At the end, we can only develop more realistic pastoral responses if we are in tune with the reality of the immigrant church in our local places of worship.

In recent years it has been so heartbreaking and painful to see a fragmented church that is allowing politics to dictate the sides and the colors of our faith. It has been so frustrating to look at a church so entangled in cheap and perverse politics. Politics so dark and so deceitful have created a divided church. Perhaps we have our eyes too fixed on politics, and that is why we do not fully embrace the mission of ministering to the displaced that God has brought to us from distant lands.

Migrants, documented or undocumented, and refugees are arriving with many wounds, broken hearts, and confused minds to a new culture. Therefore, we do not have to go out of the country or fund enormous budgets to start our mission programs. Our mission programs can start walking on the corners of the street, at the bus stop, or maybe interacting with the lady cleaning your house or the guy doing our yard. I invite you to look not at the individual who by the terms of political polarization is a criminal, terrorist, or someone who wants to steal your job. Rather, I invite you to look at the one who walks wounded, confused, and thirsty for belonging, trying to find God in the middle of this outrageous journey.

Though there are a lot of reasons why we can agree or disagree on the immigration issue, I propose that we focus our hearts and minds on one question: How can we as a church properly minister among the undocumented or immigrant community? Red or blue, left or right, let's not allow politics or any kind of distraction to deprive the church of its main purpose on earth: bringing the good news to all. Can we lift up our eyes and see higher than the borders we have created? Can we as a church forget about skin color and just deeply, intentionally, look into the hearts of those weary travelers? Can we get out of our majestic buildings and walk among those on the streets selling *elotes, paletas,* and tacos or working on the fields? Can we ask the Lord to help us understand their needs and how the power of the gospel can heal those suffering hearts? I believe we can, and we should do it pursuing God's desires of bringing all to his salvation. A God "who wants all people to be saved and to come to a knowledge of the truth" (1 Tim 2:4). Can we ask God to let us see the immigration issue from a kingdom perspective? I hope we can respond to this issue as Christians and citizens of God's kingdom. I hope the Holy Spirit can pour his compassion, love, and tolerance into us, so we can ask God to help us be the church America needs.

There is currently a superficial recognition of the needs faced by undocumented immigrants. In addition to that, there is an awareness within the American church itself about the way in which migration is bringing new people to our meeting places. Currently, there are already ministries and organizations trying to ease the burden of this very vulnerable community. However, that connection and relationship to guide and help this community has not been achieved. Perhaps it is the most challenging part of doing ministry in the margins, because it is about going and imitating what Jesus did. He walked among them, sat down with them, and showed them the healing power of the gospel.

We are the church, an expanding community capable of setting aside any race or any socioeconomic distinction. We need to continue working in synchronicity with God's purpose for our world and we need to continue being a community able to understand what God is doing, always looking to be founded on a fresh biblical perspective of mercy and justice. We need to be a community conscious enough to understand that the Holy Spirit is shaping a multiethnic church for eternity. Our destiny transcends any territorial limit; nothing can stop the advance of God's plans, not even the biggest walls or the most unpredictable deserts or jungles. God will continue moving through migration, as he always has since Genesis.

Epilogue

It is the beginning of 2025, and once again, leaders in the current political climate have labeled immigration as one of their first issues to address. This is a perfect time, then, for the church to address this issue with a perspective rooted in the kingdom of God. There is a lot of tension and nervousness within the undocumented community. The return of President Trump has put millions of Hispanics residing in the United States on alert, among them the most vulnerable: the undocumented. One of the most common comments voiced in this community is "we are worried that *la migra* will start carrying out raids." They have been living anxiously with knots in their throats since the results of the November 2024 election and comments about massive deportations. Tom Homan has once again been chosen by Trump as the "border czar." In his statements, Homan warned that to avoid the separation of families, he will deport every member of the family. The president-elect corroborated the information, and mentioned that in the case of mixed families, undocumented parents would have to make the difficult decision of taking their children with them or leaving them in the care of a guardian.

In his first speech as president, Trump revealed some of the executive orders that he had promised to deliver on the first day of his government. A dozen of these aim to fight against the disastrous invasion of the border, as Trump defines the crisis at the border to be. As announced in his campaign, the president plans to toughen the requirements to become an American, mobilize troops at the border with Mexico, declare a national emergency to reduce irregular immigration, and designate Mexican drug cartels and gangs as terrorist organizations.

In addition, Trump affirmed that he would end the practice that he classified as "catch and release," referencing an immigration policy under which immigrants who were detained when crossing the border irregularly in the United States were released while they waited for the resolution of their cases in immigration courts. President Trump has gone further, confirming that he will send troops to the border with Mexico as part of his declaration of a national emergency to contain what he calls a crisis in that part of the country. The Trump administration has also ended the use of a mobile border app called CBP One, which has allowed almost a million people to legally enter the United States with the right to work. A notice posted on January 20 on the Customs and Border Protection website informed users that the app is no longer available. The notice said existing appointments had been cancelled. At the border, there are many families crying because the opportunity to enter the country legally has been cancelled.

Meanwhile, the undocumented community tries to keep its usual routines, but with the hopeless feeling that at any moment they could be deported. Some of the families and parents that fear deportation commented, "we are going to continue working, there is no other option; if they catch me, I am not going to say anything and I am going to fight the case and defend my rights." Many have chosen to lower their profile or resign themselves to whatever comes. "If I have to stay here or be deported, it will be God's decision," are the words of some of the families who go to church every Sunday. They are visibly uncomfortable when asked about politics and immigration.

Some employers fear being inspected and have fired undocumented people, who often do the hardest and lowest-paying jobs. Currently, many migrants are struggling to find other jobs and entire families are starting to think about what's next. "If things get complicated, we will leave," are the comments of some Venezuelan families.

On the other hand, the mobilization of community and religious leaders has not stopped since the election results came out. There are many efforts to respond to the needs that this new policy will unleash in this very vulnerable community. For these leaders, it is unthinkable that we stand idly by while many families in our communities are affected and deported. It is equally unthinkable for them that we, as a nation, will witness the destruction of our historic national outreach to refugees at a time when the need to offer safe havens to refugees is growing around the world.

As Christians, we have a responsibility to heal the nation through actions of civic engagement that lie beyond the borders of political party structures and government itself. As a church, we urge citizens to follow social teaching, demonstrating sympathetic compassion for all those who are suffering amid the circumstances, combined with action. In California, the presence of the border patrol in unusual places has been reported, and all this has created a lot of fear. Many church-going families and some others in our community have expressed their fear and mentioned how their routines have changed. Some only drive from home to work; some have expressed anxiety and insomnia due to worries about being detained.

These scenarios and many other situations will take place in the next years here in the United States. Without a doubt, there will be tons of pastoral work on the margins with the most vulnerable communities. I hope, as a church, that we remember that migrants and refugees should not be seen as numbers, statistics, or threats, but as people with stories, dreams, and sufferings. I hope we recognize that each country has the right and obligation to regulate the entry of people into its territory, but always with humanity and justice. Let us continue to reiterate that migrants are not a threat, but a human reality that must be managed with solidarity and mercy. Let us be a church that welcomes, protects, accompanies, and integrates the most vulnerable.

EPILOGUE

Pilgrim, keep walking.
Pilgrim, keep dreaming.
Don't let the pain steal your breath.
Don't let suffering steal your hope.
Don't let contempt steal the value God has given you.
Remember that God loves you.

> January 20, 2025
> Inauguration Day

Notes

INTRODUCTION

1 "States Offering Drivers' Licenses to Immigrants," National Conference of States Legislatures, updated March 13, 2023, accessed January 20, 2024, https://www.ncsl.org/immigration/states-offering-drivers-licenses-to-immigrants
2 I use the term *Hispanic* throughout this book even though I do not prefer it. It comes from the word *Hispania*, a name for the Iberian Peninsula. This term still can refer to things related to Spain, but in the United States it more popularly refers to people who are of Spanish or Latin American descent.
3 Leopoldo A. Sánchez, "Hispanic Is Not What You Think," *Concordia Journal* 42, no. 3 (Summer 2016), accessed June 20, 2024, https://issuu.com/concordiasem/docs/cj_summer_2016-final_7.25.16/61. In United States the term *Hispanic* refers to a homogenous group of people with ties to Latin America. It was during the Nixon administration when this term was first adopted.
4 *Familismo*, the value of closeness and interconnectedness among family members, is prevalent in Latino culture. *Familismo* includes a sense of family obligation, respect for elders, and a sense of responsibility and obligation to care for all members of the family. *Familismo* and extended kin give the task of raising children a sense of community. Latino Cultural Guide, accessed January 20, 2024, https://conservancy.umn.edu/server/api/core/bitstreams/5c915812-3272-41f6-b549-f2fa23ce9a35/content.
5 *Personalismo*, personal connectedness in interactions, refers to the high level of emotional resonance and personal involvement with family encounters or friends in Latino culture. Lisa Fortuna, "Working with Latino/a and Hispanic Patients," American Psychiatric Association, accessed January 20, 2024, https://www.psychiatry.org/psychiatrists/diversity/education/best-practice-highlights/working-with-latino-patients
6 *Respeto* refers to how Latino cultures tend to give greater deference and respect to individuals operating according to a clearly defined social hierarchy where kids defer to adults and adults defer to elders. American Psychological Association, "Cultural Considerations," *Monitor on Psychology* 36,

no. 1 (January 2005), accessed January 20, 2024, https://www.apa.org/monitor/jan05/considerations
7. George W. Bush, *On The Issues Immigration*, 2000, accessed January 23, 2024, https://www.4president.org//issues/bush2000/bush2000immigration.htm
8. In 1986, the US Congress approved the Immigration Reform and Control Act (IRCA), the last reform that considered the mass regularization of undocumented immigrants. The IRCA has allowed more than three million people to be regularized, most of them Mexican.
9. Pew Research Center, *Facts on U.S. Immigrants*, 2018, accessed January 23, 2024, https://www.pewresearch.org/hispanic/2020/08/20/facts-on-u-s-immigrants/. The undocumented population declined to 10.5 million, in 2017. Mexicans make up less than half of that population.
10. Ruth M. Melkonian-Hoover and Lyman A. Kellstedt, *Evangelicals and Immigration Fault Lines Among the Faithful* (Palgrave Macmillan, 2019), 43.
11. Melkonian-Hoover and Kellstedt, *Evangelicals and Immigration*, 44.
12. "How America's Faith Has Changed Since 9-11," Barna, November 26, 2001, https://www.barna.com/research/how-americas-faith-has-changed-since-9-11/
13. Melkonian-Hoover and Kellstedt, *Evangelicals and Immigration*, 43–44.
14. Miguel A. De La Torre, *Trails of Hope and Terror: Testimonies on Immigration* (Orbis Books, 2009), 5.
15. Romal, J. Tune, "Does the Black Church Support Immigration Reform? A Conversation with Bishop Vashti McKenzie, African Methodist Episcopal Church," *HuffPost*, May 21, 2010, https://www.huffpost.com/entry/does-the-black-church-sup_b_507589
16. Melkonian-Hoover and Kellstedt, *Evangelicals and Immigration*, 75.
17. Mark R. Amstutz, *Just Immigration: American Policy in Christian Perspective* (Eerdmans, 2017), 171.
18. SBC, *On Immigration and the Gospel*, June 1, 2011, https://www.sbc.net/resource-library/resolutions/on-immigration-and-the-gospel/
19. CRCNA, *Committee to Study the Migration of Workers*, accessed February 6, 2024, https://www.crcna.org/sites/default/files/Migration.pdf
20. "About Evangelical Immigration Table," Evangelical Immigration Table, accessed February 6, 2024, https://evangelicalimmigrationtable.com/about/#PRINCIPLES
21. Joseph Castleberry, *The New Pilgrims: How Immigrants Are Renewing America's Faith and Values* (Worthy Publishing, 2015), 251.
22. "President Barack Obama and the Hispanic Community," The White House President Barack Obama, accessed February 6, 2024, https://obamawhitehouse.archives.gov/hispanic
23. Melkonian-Hoover and Kellstedt, *Evangelicals and Immigration*, 45.
24. Dale Hanson Bourke, *Immigration: Tough Questions, Direct Answers* (InterVarsity Press, 2014), 73.

25 Hanson Bourke, *Immigration*, 74.
26 Melkonian-Hoover and Kellstedt, *Evangelicals and Immigration*, 47.
27 Hanson Bourke, *Immigration*, 77.
28 US Customs and Border Protection, *Southwest Border Unaccompanied Alien Children* FY 2014, accessed January 30, 2024, https://www.cbp.gov/newsroom/stats/southwest-border-unaccompanied-children/fy-2014
29 Melkonian-Hoover and Kellstedt, *Evangelicals and Immigration*, 55.
30 "Trump Says Mexico Sending 'Rapists' Across Border; He'd Make Country Pay for Border Wall" Fox News, June 16, 2016, accessed February 1, 2024, https://www.foxnews.com/politics/trump-says-mexico-sending-rapists-across-border-hed-make-country-pay-for-border-wall
31 Fathali M. Moghaddam and Margaret J. Hendricks, *Contemporary Immigration: Psychological Perspectives to Address Challenges and inform Solutions* (American Psychological Association, 2022), 5.
32 Pratyusha Tummala-Narra, *Trauma and Racial Minority Immigrants: Turmoil, Uncertainty, and Resistance* (American Psychological Association, 2021), 5.
33 Melkonian-Hoover and Kellstedt, *Evangelicals and Immigration*, 55.
34 David Roach, "A Year After the Election, Trump's Effect on Evangelical Churches Lingers," *Christianity Today*, November 1, 2021, https://www.christianitytoday.com/news/2021/november/trump-effects-evangelical-churches-witness-survey-election.html
35 Brad Christerson et al., *God's Resistance: Mobilizing Faith to Defend Immigrants* (New York Press, 2024), 31.
36 PCUSA, *Resolution Calling for a Comprehensive Legalization Program for Immigrants Living and Working in the United States*, accessed January 20, 2024, https://pcusa.org/resource/resolution-calling-comprehensive-legalization-program-immigrants-living-and-working-united-states
37 PCUSA, "Presbyterians Urged to Speak Out for Millions of Undocumented People" accessed March 20, 2025, https://pcusa.org/news-storytelling/news/2021/7/26/presbyterians-urged-speak-out-millions-undocumented-people
38 "The Acts of Convention," The Archives of the Episcopal Church, accessed January 20, 2024, https://www.episcopalarchives.org/cgi-bin/acts/acts_resolution.pl?resolution=2006-A017
39 "House of Bishops Issues Pastoral Letter Along with a Theological Resource: *The Nation and the Common Good: Reflections on Immigration Reform*," The Episcopal Church, accessed January 20, 2024, https://www.episcopalchurch.org/publicaffairs/house-of-bishops-issues-pastoral-letter-along-with-a-theological-resource-%C2%93the-nation-and-the-common-good-reflections-on-immigration-reform%C2%94/amp/
40 Amstutz, *Just Immigration*, 202.
41 David A. Badillo, *Latinos and the New Immigrant Church* (Johns Hopkins University Press, 2006), 193.

42 Moghaddam and Hendricks, *Contemporary Immigration*, 5–6.
43 Moghaddam and Hendricks, *Contemporary Immigration*, 184.
44 J. Baxter Oliphant and Andy Cerda, "Republicans and Democrats Have Different Top Priorities for U.S. Immigration Policy, Pew Research Center, accessed January 16, 2024, https://www.pewresearch.org/fact-tank/2022/09/08/republicans-and-democrats-have-different-top-priorities-for-u-s-immigration-policy/
45 "The Religious Affiliation of U.S. Immigrants: Majority Christian, Rising Share of Other Faiths, Pew Research Center, accessed January 17, 2024, https://www.pewresearch.org/religion/2013/05/17/the-religious-affiliation-of-us-immigrants/
46 Badillo, *Latinos and the New Immigrant Church*, 183.
47 Badillo, *Latinos and the New Immigrant Church*, 185.
48 "Among U.S. Latinos, Catholicism Continues to Decline but Is Still the Largest Faith," Pew Research Center, accessed January 19, 2024, https://www.pewresearch.org/religion/2023/04/13/among-u-s-latinos-catholicism-continues-to-decline-but-is-still-the-largest-faith/
49 Castleberry, *The New Pilgrims*, 29.
50 "The Global Religious Landscape," Pew Research Center, accessed May 18, 2024, https://www.pewresearch.org/religion/2012/12/18/global-religious-landscape-exec/
51 M. McAuliffe and A. Triandafyllidou, eds. *World Migration Report 2022*. International Organization for Migration (IOM), accessed January 16, 2024, https://publications.iom.int/books/world-migration-report-2022
52 Tummala-Narra, *Trauma and Racial Minority Immigrants*, 4.
53 Moghaddam and Hendricks, *Contemporary Immigration*, 185.
54 American Immigration Council, *Immigrants in the United States*, accessed January 17, 2024, https://www.americanimmigrationcouncil.org/research/immigrants-in-the-united-states
55 John Gramlich and Alissa Scheller, "What's Happening at the US-Mexico Border in 7 Charts," Pew Research Center, accessed March 20, 2025, https://www.pewresearch.org/short-reads/2021/11/09/whats-happening-at-the-u-s-mexico-border-in-7-charts/
56 "Crossing the Darién Gap: Migrants Risk Death on the Journey to the U.S.," Council on Foreign Relations, accessed May 20, 2024 https://www.cfr.org/article/crossing-darien-gap-migrants-risk-death-journey-us
57 For more details about this migration route, watch this video at: https://www.cbsnews.com/news/darien-gap-dead-end-desperate-journey/

CHAPTER 1: DEFINING THE IMMIGRANT COMMUNITY

1 Lee M. Penyak and Walter J. Petry, *Religion and Society in Latin America: Interpretive Essays from Conquest to Present* (Orbis Books, 2009), 63.

NOTES

2   Elizondo Virgilio, *Galilean Journey: The Mexican-American Promise* (Orbis Books, 2000), 10.
3   Penyak and Petry, *Religion and Society in Latin America*, 83.
4   Penyak and Petry, *Religion and Society in Latin America*, 95.
5   Virgilio, *Galilean Journey*, 12.
6   Penyak and Petry, *Religion and Society in Latin America*, 78.
7   José Vasconcelos, *La Raza Cósmica* (Editorial Porrúa, 2019), 33.
8   Virgilio, *Galilean Journey*, 10.
9   John F. Kennedy, *A Nation of Immigrants* (Harper Perennial, 2018), 13–20.
10 Elizondo, *Galilean Journey*, 14.
11 Juan Francisco Martinez, *The Story of Latino Protestants in the United States* (Eerdmans, 2018), 27.
12 Virgilio, *Galilean Journey*, 15.
13 Gaston Espinoza et al., *Latino Religious and Civic Activism in the United States* (Oxford University Press, 2005), 28–29.
14 Gerald D. Jaynes, *Immigration and Race: New Challenges for American Democracy* (Yale University Press, 2000), 7.
15 Kennedy, *A Nation of Immigrants*, 41.
16 Kennedy, *A Nation of Immigrants*, 42.
17 "Immigration and the American Church: A Remix," Anxious Bench, accessed May 26, 2024, https://www.patheos.com/blogs/anxiousbench/2022/01/immigration-and-the-american-church-a-remix/
18 Alex D. Montoya, *Hispanic Ministry in North America* (Zondervan, 1987), 11.
19 "Subject definitions," US Census Bureau, accessed May 26, 2024, https://www.census.gov/programs-surveys/cps/technical-documentation/subject-definitions.html#ethnicorigin
20 Raul Zaldivar et al., *El Rostro Hispano de Jesús una Visión Cultural, Pastoral y Social* (Editorial Clie, 2014), 24–27.
21 "Central American Immigrants in the United States," MPI, accessed May 21, 2024, https://www.migrationpolicy.org/article/central-american-immigrants-united-states
22 "South American Immigrants in the United States," MPI, accessed May 27, 2024: https://www.migrationpolicy.org/article/south-american-immigrants-united-states
23 MPI, "South American Immigrants in the United States."
24 "Facts on Hispanics of Mexican Origin in the United States, 2021," Pew Research Center, accessed September 20, 2024: https://www.pewresearch.org/race-and-ethnicity/fact-sheet/us-hispanics-facts-on-mexican-origin.
25 Raquel Rosenbloom and Jeanne Batalova, "Mexican Immigrants in the United States," MPI, accessed September 20, 2024, https://www.migrationpolicy.org/article/mexican-immigrants-united-states-2021.
26 "Eight Hispanic Groups Each Had a Million or More Population in 2020," US Census Bureau, accessed May 28, 2024, https://www.census.gov/library/stories/2023/09/2020-census-dhc-a-hispanic-population.html.

27 Montoya, *Hispanic Ministry in North America*, 12.
28 "8 Facts About Recent Latino Immigrants to the U.S.," Pew Research Center, accessed May 18, https://www.pewresearch.org/short-reads/2023/09/28/8-facts-about-recent-latino-immigrants-to-the-us/
29 "Generational Differences," Pew Research Center, accessed May 19, 2024, https://www.pewresearch.org/race-and-ethnicity/2004/03/19/generational-differences/.
30 "The Ways Hispanics Describe Their Identity Vary Across Immigrant Generations," Pew Research Center, accessed on September 14, 2024, https://www.pewresearch.org/short-reads/2020/09/24/the-ways-hispanics-describe-their-identity-vary-across-immigrant-generations/
31 "A Portrait of Unauthorized Immigrants in the United States," Pew Research Center, accessed May 22, 2024, https://www.pewresearch.org/hispanic/2009/04/14/a-portrait-of-unauthorized-immigrants-in-the-united-states/
32 A person who empirically treats bone dislocations and performs massages to relieve certain muscle problems. Even in some areas of Mexico there is a tendency to magnify the abilities of these people, more than those of a doctor.
33 Pew Research Center, "A Portrait of Unauthorized Immigrants in the United States."
34 *The language of heaven* is a very common phrase among Hispanics, which emphasizes the beauty and linguistic richness of the Spanish language.
35 Montoya, *Hispanic Ministry*, 11.
36 Eva Juarros-Daussa, "El Spanglish," accessed July 27, 2024, http://www.ub.edu/diccionarilinguistica/print/350.
37 Montoya, *Hispanic Ministry*, 21.
38 Martinez, *The Story of Latino Protestants in the United States*, 167.
39 Montoya, *Hispanic Ministry*, 14.
40 Irene Bloemraad, "The Debate over Multiculturalism: Philosophy, Politics, and Policy," MPI, accessed September 7, 2024, https://www.migrationpolicy.org/article/debate-over-multiculturalism-philosophy-politics-and-policy
41 Juan Francisco Martinez, *Walk with the People: Latino Ministry in the United States* (Wipf and Stock, 2016), 21
42 Ismael Garcia, *Dignidad: Ethics Through Hispanics Eyes* (Abingdon Press, 1997), 24.
43 Montoya, *Hispanic Ministry*, 18.
44 Garcia, *Dignidad*, 23.
45 Martinez, *Walk with the People*, 17.
46 Ken R. Crane, *Latino Churches: Faith, Family, and Ethnicity in the Second Generation* (LFB Scholarly Publishing, 2010), 8.
47 Per Merriam-Webster, *Don Juan* refers to a legendary Spaniard proverbial for his seduction of women, a captivating man known as a great lover or seducer of women.

48 Montoya, *Hispanic Ministry*, 19–20.
49 Martinez, *The Story of Latino Protestants in the United States*, 99–108.
50 Celia Jaes Falicov, *Latino Families in Therapy* (The Guilford Press, 2014), 65.
51 Castleberry, *The New Pilgrims*, 28.
52 Castleberry, *The New Pilgrims*, 29.
53 M. Daniel Carroll R., *Christians at the Border: Immigration, the Church, and the Bible* (Brazos Press, 2013), 35.
54 Castleberry, *The New Pilgrims*, 33.
55 Carroll R., *Christians at the Border*, 37.
56 Martinez, *The Story of Latino Protestants in the United States*, 131.
57 Martinez, *The Story of Latino Protestants in the United States*, 153.

CHAPTER 2: A THEOLOGY THAT INVITES IMMIGRANTS INTO BELONGING

1 Virgilio Elizondo, *Galilean Journey*, 15–30.
2 Justo L. Gonzalez, *Mañana: Christian Theology from a Hispanic Perspective* (Abingdon Press, 1990), 55–74.
3 Carroll R., *Christians at the Border*, 42.
4 Daniel G. Groody, *A Theology of Migration: The Bodies of Refugees and the Body of Christ* (Orbis Books, 2022), 297–300.
5 Cláudio Carvalhaes, *Liturgies from Below: Praying with People at the End of the World* (Abingdon Press, 2020), 7–15.
6 Leopoldo Sánchez, "The Migrant Face of the Church: The Church Catholic in an Age of Migration," *Putting a Human Face to Migration*, conference hosted by Calvin Institute of Worship, June 2024.
7 Justo Gonzalez, interview by the author, Predicación y Adoración, Liturgia en Nuestras Iglesias, November 2014.
8 Javier Zamora, *Solito: A Memoir* (Hogarth, 2022). This book has become a *New York Times* bestseller; for more details visit https://www.amazon.com/Solito-Memoir-Javier-Zamora/dp/0593498062.
9 Erika L. Sánchez, *I Am Not Your Perfect Mexican Daughter* (Ember, 2019). This book has won several awards. For more details visit: https://erikalsanchez.com/i-am-not-your-perfect-mexican-daughter.
10 This book is considered a national bestseller, many universities have adopted it as their freshman or common reading. For more details visit: http://enriquesjourney.com/
11 Tisha M. Rejendra, *Migrants and Citizens: Justice and Responsibility in the Ethics of Immigration* (Eerdmans, 2017), 4–5.
12 Rejendra, *Migrants and Citizens*, 13.
13 Groody, *A Theology of Migration*, 24.
14 J. D. Payne, *Strangers Next Door: Immigration, Migration and Mission* (InterVarsity Press, 2012), 28–29.

NOTES

15 Groody, *A Theology of Migration*, 26.
16 Kent Annan, *You Welcomed Me: Loving Refugees and Immigrants Because God First Loved Us* (InterVarsity Press, 2018), 7.
17 Groody, *A Theology of Migration*, 28.
18 Annan, *You Welcomed Me*, 6.
19 Groody, *A Theology of Migration*, 30.
20 In its *Glossary on Migration*, the International Organization for Migration defines the terms related to migration as follows: *Immigrant*—"From the perspective of the country of arrival, a person who moves into a country other than that of his or her nationality or usual residence, so that the country of destination effectively becomes his or her new country of usual residence." *Undocumented migrant*—"A non-national who enters or stays in a country without the appropriate documentation." *Undocumented migrant worker*—"A migrant who is not authorized to enter, to stay and to engage in a remunerated activity in the State of employment pursuant to the law of that State and to international agreements to which that State is a party." Alice Sironi et al., eds., *Glossary on Migration*. International Migration Law, no. 34. International Organization for Migration (IOM), 2019.
21 Annan, *You Welcomed Me*, 16.
22 Annan, *You Welcomed Me*, 19.
23 Carroll R., *Christians at the Border*, 46.
24 Payne, *Strangers Next Door*, 68.
25 Carroll R., *Christians at the Border*, 47.
26 Groody, *A Theology of Migration*, 22.
27 Carroll R., *Christians at the Border*, 47.
28 Castleberry, *The New Pilgrims*, 46.
29 Groody, *A Theology of Migration*, 67.
30 Payne, *Strangers Next Door*, 69.
31 Groody, *A Theology of Migration*, 72.
32 Carroll R., *Christians at the Border*, 60.
33 Carroll R., *Christians at the Border*, 44–45.
34 Matthew Soerens and Jenny Yang, *Welcoming the Stranger: Justice, Compassion and Truth in the Immigration Debate* (InterVarsity Press, 2009), 111.
35 Groody, *A Theology of Migration*, 86.
36 M. Daniel Carroll R., *The Bible and Borders: Hearing God's Word on Immigration* (Brazos Press, 2020), 35–37.
37 Carroll R., *Christians at the Border*, 68.
38 Castleberry, *The New Pilgrims*, 49.
39 Groody, *A Theology of Migration*, 132.
40 Soerens and Yang, *Welcoming the Stranger*, 92.
41 Groody, *A Theology of Migration*, 146.

42 Augustine of Hippo, *City of God*, ed. and trans. Henry Bettenson (Penguin Group, 1972), 878.
43 Bible Hub, 1 Peter, accessed January 12, 2023, https://biblehub.com/greek/3941.htm
44 Carroll R., *Christians at the Border*, 117.
45 Soerens and Yang, *Welcoming the Stranger*, 95.
46 Robert W. Heimburger, *God and the Illegal Alien: United States Immigration Law and a Theology of Politics* (Cambridge University Press, 2018), 44–94.
47 Dana W. Wilbanks, *Re-Creating America: The Ethics of U.S. Immigration and Refugee Policy in a Christian Perspective* (Abingdon Press, 1996), 75.
48 Castleberry, *The New Pilgrims*, 36.
49 Heimburger, *God and the Illegal Alien*, 36.
50 Soerens and Yang, *Welcoming the Stranger*, 86.
51 Castleberry, *The New Pilgrims*, 36.
52 Heimburger, *God and the Illegal Alien*, 36.
53 In this context, this phrase means that we have an abundance of theological material regarding immigration.
54 Simon C. Kim, *An Immigration of Theology: Theology of Context as the Theological Method of Virgilio Elizondo and Gustavo Gutierrez* (Pickwick Publications, 2012), 100.
55 Kim, *An Immigration of Theology*, 103.
56 Heimburger, *God and the Illegal Alien*, 59.
57 João B. Chavez, *Migrational Religion: Context and Creativity in the Latinx Diaspora* (Baylor University Press, 2021), 81.
58 Eugene Cho and Samira Izadi Page, *No Longer Strangers* (Eerdmans, 2021), 25.
59 Mother Teresa, *No Greater Love* (MJF Books, 1989), 69–72.
60 Harold J. Recinos, *Who Comes in the Name of the Lord: Jesus at the Margins* (Abingdon Press, 1997), 32.
61 Pope Francis, *Open Mind, Faithful Heart: Reflections on Following Jesus* (Crossroad Publishing, 2013), 171–172.

CHAPTER 3: PSYCHOLOGICAL NEEDS IN THE IMMIGRANT COMMUNITY

1 Anthony J. Marsella et al., *Amidst Peril and Pain: The Mental Well Being of the Worlds Refugees* (American Psychological Association, 1994), 158.
2 Falicov, *Latino Families in Therapy*, 78–79.
3 Daniel Groody and Giancchino Campese, *A Promised Land, a Perilous Journey: Theological Perspectives on Migration* (University of Notre Dame Press, 2008), 108–110.
4 Hanson Bourke, *Immigration*, 40.

NOTES

5 Jaes Falicov, *Latino Families in Therapy*, 81–85.
6 Shaun Wiley et al., *Social Categories in Everyday Experience* (American Psychological Association, 2012), 4.
7 Charles F. Kemp, *Pastoral Care with the Poor* (Abingdon Press, 1972), 42
8 Daniel Sanchez, *Hispanic Realities Impacting America: Implications for Evangelism and Missions* (Church Starting Network, 2006), 103.
9 Wiley et al., *Social Categories in Everyday Experience*, 12.
10 Cho and Page, *No Longer Strangers*, 88.
11 Wiley et al., *Social Categories in Everyday Experience*, 13.
12 Sanchez, *Hispanic Realities Impacting America*, 97.
13 Wiley et al., *Social Categories in Everyday Experience*, 20.
14 Sanchez, *Hispanic Realities Impacting America*, 99.
15 Wiley et al., *Social Categories in Everyday Experience*, 13.
16 Sanchez, *Hispanic Realities Impacting America*, 102.
17 Wiley et al., *Social Categories in Everyday Experience*, 14.
18 Kemp, *Pastoral Care with the Poor*, 38.
19 Jeseba Achotegui, Migration and Mental Health, The Ulysses Syndrome, accessed September 20, 2024, https://hia.berkeley.edu/wp-content/uploads/2018/12/deuils-migratoires-syndrome-dulysse-en.pdf
20 Kemp, *Pastoral Care with the Poor*, 40.
21 Leon Grinberg and Rebeca Grinberg, *Psychoanalytic Perspectives on Migration and Exile* (Yale University Press, 1989), 67.
22 Marsella et al., *Amidst Peril and Pain*, 158.
23 Grinberg, *Psychoanalytic Perspectives on Migration and Exile*, 79.
24 Marsella et al., *Amidst Peril and Pain*, 160.
25 Moghaddam and Hendricks, *Contemporary Immigration*, 5.
26 Grinberg, *Psychoanalytic Perspectives on Migration and Exile*, 85.
27 Tummala-Narra, *Trauma and Racial Minority Immigrants*, 33.
28 Tummala-Narra, *Trauma and Racial Minority Immigrants*, 34.
29 Tummala-Narra, *Trauma and Racial Minority Immigrants*, 36.
30 Tummala-Narra, *Trauma and Racial Minority Immigrants*, 39.
31 Tummala-Narra, *Trauma and Racial Minority Immigrants*, 41.
32 Tummala-Narra, *Trauma and Racial Minority Immigrants*, 44.
33 Marsella et al., *Amidst Peril and Pain*, 194.
34 Marsella, et al., *Amidst Peril and Pain*, 196.
35 American Psychiatric Association, *Diagnostic and Statistical Manual of Mental Disorders*, 5th ed., text rev. (DSM-5-TR) (American Psychiatric Association, 2022), 312.
36 Marsella et al., *Amidst Peril and Pain*, 198.
37 American Psychiatric Association, DSM-5-TR, 301–305.
38 Cho and Page, *No Longer Strangers*, 32–35.
39 American Psychiatric Association, DSM-5-TR, 295.
40 Cho and Page, *No Longer Strangers*, 37.
41 Recinos, *Who Comes in the Name of the Lord*, 143.

CHAPTER 4: PASTORAL CARE IN THE MARGINS

1. Daniel A. Rodriguez, *A Future for the Latino Church: Models for Multilingual, Multigenerational Hispanic Congregations* (InterVarsity Press, 2011), 122.
2. Henry. J. M. Nouwen, *In the Name of Jesus: Reflections on Christian Leadership* (Crossroad, 1989), 81.
3. Henry. J. M. Nouwen, *The Wounded Healer* (Bantam Doubleday Dell, 1972), 91.
4. Mark Deymaz, *Disruption: Repurposing the Church to Redeem the Community* (Harper Collins, 2017), 13.
5. Groody and Campese, *A Promised Land*, 113.
6. Henri, J. M. Nouwen, *The Return of the Prodigal Son: A Story of Homecoming* (Doubleday, 1994), 39.
7. Henri, J. M. Nouwen, *Discernment* (Harper Collins, 2013), 85.
8. Groody and Campese, *A Promised Land*, 148.
9. Groody and Campese, *A Promised Land*, 149.
10. Cho and Page, *No Longer Strangers*, 71.
11. "L.A. Churches Promise Sanctuary for Migrant Families as ICE Raids Begin Sunday," KTLA 5 News, accessed November 12, 2024, https://ktla.com/news/local-news/l-a-churches-promise-sanctuary-for-migrant-families-as-ice-raids-begin-sunday/
12. Groody and Campese, *A Promised Land*, 148–152.
13. Kemp, *Pastoral Care with the Poor*, 71.
14. Donald Kerwin and Jill Marie Gerschut, *And You Welcomed Me: Migration and Catholic Social Teaching*, (Lexington Books/Fortress Academic, 2009), 127.
15. Sanchez, *Hispanic Realities Impacting America*, 103.
16. Kerwin and Gerschut, *And You Welcomed Me*, 131.
17. Kemp, *Pastoral Care with the Poor*, 68.
18. Sanchez, *Hispanic Realities Impacting America*, 90.
19. Sanchez, *Hispanic Realities Impacting America*, 91.
20. "Staten Island Church Pursuing Migrant Shelter," Spectrum News NY1, accessed November 12, 2024, https://ny1.com/nyc/staten-island/news/2024/01/19/staten-island-church-pursuing-migrant-shelter
21. "Affordable Housing on Church Parking Lots? A New Law Makes it Easier to Build," *Los Angeles Times*, accessed November 12, 2024, https://www.latimes.com/california/story/2024-09-01/affordable-housing-on-church-parking-lots-new-laws-make-it-easier-to-build#:~:text=A%20California%20law%20that%20went,built%20in%20single%2Dfamily%20neighborhoods
22. Deymaz, *Disruption*, 87.
23. Timothy Keller, *Generous Justice: How God's Grace Makes Us Just* (Penguin Books, 2016), 3.

NOTES

24 Christopher L. Heuertz and Christine D. Pohl, *Friendship at the Margins: Discovering Mutuality in Service and Mission* (InterVarsity Press, 2010), 52.
25 "Distribution of Total Population and Poverty by Race Using the Official Poverty Measure: 2022," US Census Bureau, accessed May 4, 2024, https://www.census.gov/content/dam/Census/library/visualizations/2023/demo/p60-280/figure3.pdf
26 Sanchez, *Hispanic Realities Impacting America*, 45.
27 Sanchez, *Hispanic Realities Impacting America*, 94.
28 Groody and Campese, *A Promised Land*, 155–156.

Bibliography

American Psychiatric Association. *Diagnostic and Statistical Manual of Mental Disorders*. 5th ed., text rev. (DSM-5-TR). American Psychiatric Association, 2022.
Amstutz, Mark R. *Just Immigration: American Policy in Christian Perspective*. Eerdmans, 2017.
Annan, Kent. *You Welcomed Me: Loving Refugees and Immigrants Because God First Loved Us*. InterVarsity Press, 2018.
Augustine of Hippo. *City of God*, edited and translated by Henry Bettenson. Penguin Group, 1972.
Badillo, David A. *Latinos and the New Immigrant Church*. Johns Hopkins University Press, 2006.
Bauman, Stephan, Matthew Soerens, and Issam Smeir. *Seeking Refuge: On the Shores of the Global Refugee Crisis*. Moody Publishers, 2016.
Carroll R., M. Daniel. *The Bible and Borders: Hearing God's Word on Immigration*. Brazos Press, 2020.
Carroll R., M. Daniel. *Christians at the Border: Immigration, the Church, and the Bible*. Brazos Press, 2013.
Carvalhaes, Cláudio. *Liturgies from Below: Praying with People at the End of the World*. Abingdon Press, 2020.
Castleberry, Joseph. *The New Pilgrims: How Immigrants Are Renewing America's Faith and Values*. Worthy Publishing, 2015.
Chavez, João B. *Migrational Religion: Context and Creativity in the Latinx Diaspora*. Baylor University Press, 2021.
Cho, Eugene, and Samira Izadi Page. *No Longer Strangers*. Eerdmans, 2021.
Christerson, Brad, Alexia Salvatierra, Robert Chao Romero, and Nancy Wang Yuen. *God's Resistance: Mobilizing Faith to Defend Immigrants*. New York University Press, 2024.
Crane, Ken R. *Latino Churches: Faith, Family, and Ethnicity in the Second Generation*. LFB Scholarly Publishing, 2010.

De La Torre, Miguel A. *Trails of Hope and Terror: Testimonies on Immigration.* Orbis Books, 2009.

Deymaz, Mark. *Disruption: Repurposing the Church to Redeem the Community.* Harper Collins, 2017.

Elizondo, Virgilio. *Galilean Journey: The Mexican-American Promise.* Orbis Books, 2000.

Espinoza, Gaston, Virgilio Elizondo, and Jesse Miranda, eds. *Latino Religious and Civic Activism in the United States.* Oxford University Press, 2005.

Falicov, Celia Jaes. *Latino Families in Therapy.* The Guilford Press, 2014.

Francis. *Open Mind, Faithful Heart: Reflections on Following Jesus.* Crossroad, 2013.

Gonzalez, Justo L. *Mañana: Christian Theology from a Hispanic Perspective.* Abingdon Press, 1990.

Grinberg, Leon, and Rebecca Grinberg. *Psychoanalytic Perspectives on Migration and Exile.* Yale University Press, 1989.

Groody, Daniel G. *A Theology of Migration: The Bodies of Refugees and the Body of Christ.* Orbis Books, 2022.

Groody, Daniel G., and Gianchhino Campese. *A Promised Land, a Perilous Journey: Theological Perspectives on Migration.* University of Notre Dame Press, 2008.

Hanson Bourke, Dale. *Immigration: Tough Questions, Direct Answers.* InterVarsity Press, 2014.

Heimburger, Robert W. *God and the Illegal Alien: United States Immigration Law and a Theology of Politics.* Cambridge University Press, 2018.

Heuertz, Christopher, and Christine D. Pohl. *Friendship at the Margins: Discovering Mutuality in Service and Mission.* InterVarsity Press, 2010.

Jaynes, Gerald David. *Immigration and Race: New Challenges for American Democracy.* Yale University Press, 2000.

Keller, Timothy. *Generous Justice: How God's Grace Makes Us Just.* Penguin Books, 2016.

Kemp, Charles F. *Pastoral Care with the Poor.* Abingdon Press, 1972.

Kennedy, John F. *A Nation of Immigrants.* Harper Perennial, 2018.

Kerwin, Donald, and Jill Marie Gerschut. *And You Welcomed Me: Migration and Catholic Social Teaching.* Lexington Books/Fortress Academic, 2009.

Kim, Simon C. *An Immigration of Theology: Theology of Context as the Theological Method of Virgilio Elizondo and Gustavo Gutiérrez.* Pickwick Publications, 2012.

Marsella, Anthony J., Thomas Bornemann, Solvig Ekblad, and John Orley. *Amidst Peril and Pain: The Mental Health and Well-Being of the World's Refugees*. American Psychological Association, 1994.

Martinez, Juan Francisco. *The Story of Latino Protestants in the United States*. Eerdmans, 2018.

Martinez, Juan Francisco. *Walk with the People: Latino Ministry in the United States*. Wipf and Stock, 2016.

Melkokian-Hoover, Ruth M., and Lyman A. Kellstedt. *Evangelicals and Immigration: Fault Lines Among the Faithful*. Oxford University Press, 2019.

Moghaddam, Fathali M., and Margeret J. Hendricks. *Contemporary Immigration: Psychological Perspectives to Address Challenges and Inform Solutions*. American Psychological Association, 2022.

Montoya, Alex D. *Hispanic Ministry in North America*. Zondervan, 1987.

Nouwen, Henri J. M. *Discernment*. Harper Collins, 2013.

Nouwen, Henri J. M. *In the Name of Jesus: Reflections on Christian Leadership*. Crossroad, 1989.

Nouwen, Henri J. M. *The Return of the Prodigal Son: A Story of Homecoming*. Doubleday, 1994.

Nouwen, Henri J. M. *The Wounded Healer*. Bantam Doubleday Dell, 1972.

Payne, J. D. *Strangers Next Door: Immigration, Migration and Mission*. InterVarsity Press, 2012.

Penyak, Lee M., and Walter J. Petry. *Religion and Society in Latin America: Interpretive Essays from Conquest to Present*. Orbis Books, 2009.

Recinos, Harold J. *Who Comes in the Name of the Lord: Jesus at the Margins*. Abingdon Press, 1997.

Rejendra, Tisha M. *Migrants and Citizens: Justice and Responsibility in the Ethics of Immigration*. Eerdmans, 2017.

Rodriguez, Daniel A. *A Future for the Latino Church: Models for Multilingual, Multigenerational Hispanic Congregations*. InterVarsity Press, 2011.

Sanchez, Daniel. *Hispanic Realities Impacting America: Implications for Evangelism and Missions*. Church Starting Network, 2006.

Sironi, Alice, Céline Bauloz, and Milen Emmanuel, eds. *Glossary on Migration*. International Migration Law, no. 34. International Organization for Migration (IOM), 2019.

Soerens, Matthew, and Jenny Yang. *Welcoming the Stranger: Justice, Compassion and Truth in the Immigration Debate*. InterVarsity Press, 2009.

Teresa, Saint (Mother). *No Greater Love*. MJF Books, 1989.

Tummala-Narra, Pratyusha. *Trauma and Racial Minority Immigrants: Turmoil, Uncertainty, and Resistance*. American Psychological Association, 2021.

Vasconcelos, José. *La Raza Cósmica*. Editorial Porrúa, 2019.
Wilbanks, Dana W. *Re-Creating America: The Ethics of U.S. Immigration and Refugee Policy in a Christian Perspective*. Abingdon Press, 1996.
Wiley, Shaun, Gina Philogene, and Tracey A. Revenson. *Social Categories in Everyday Experience*. American Psychological Association, 2012.
Zaldivar, Raul, Miguel Alvarez, and Daniel E. Ramirez. *El Rostro Hispano de Jesús una Visión Cultural, Pastoral y Social*. Editorial Clie, 2014.

www.ingramcontent.com/pod-product-compliance
Ingram Content Group UK Ltd.
Pitfield, Milton Keynes, MK11 3LW, UK
UKHW010259131125
465008UK00003B/121